ELECTRIC MUSIC

John Jenkins
and Jon Smith

ELECTRIC MUSIC

A Practical Manual

INDIANA UNIVERSITY PRESS
Bloomington   London

Manufactured in the United States of America

Library of Congress Cataloging in Publication Data

Jenkins, John, 1936–
  Electric music.

  Includes index.
  1. Musical instruments, Electronic. 2. Music—
Acoustics and physics. I. Smith, Jon, 1946–   joint
author. II. Title.
ML1092.J45   781.9'1   75–18233
ISBN 0–253–31944–7
ISBN 0–253–20195–0 paper   2 3 4 5 80 79 78 77

CONTENTS

LIST OF ILLUSTRATIONS

PLATES

The above plates are reproduced in this book, on the pages noted, by kind permission of the following: R. D. Andrews & Al Barnes, Paignton, Devon, p 119; Boosey and Hawkes (Sales) Ltd, Deansbrook Road, Edgware, Middlesex, p 102; Dallas Arbiter Ltd,

LIST OF ILLUSTRATIONS

Dallas Building, Clifton Street, London EC2P 2JR, p 35; Dana Laboratories Inc, Irvine, California, USA, p 101; Dubreq Studios Ltd, Cricklewood, London NW2 6NX, p 102; Electronic Music Studios (London) Ltd, 277 Putney Bridge Road, London SW15 2PT, p 120; Hammond Organ Company, p 101; Industrial Tape Applications, 5 Pratt Street, London NW1, p 51; Millbank Electronics Group, Uckfield, Sussex, p 34; Rupert Neve & Co Ltd, Cambridge House, Melbourne, Royston, Hertfordshire SG8 6AU, p 52; Sound Advice Installations Co Ltd, 358 Preston Road, Standish, Wigan, Lancashire, p 51; Watkins Electric Music, 66 Offley Road, London SW9 0LU, pp 33 and 34.

IN TEXT

LIST OF ILLUSTRATIONS

AUTHORS' ACKNOWLEDGEMENT

We should like to thank Dr Robert A. Moog of New York for reading the draft manuscript and making several valuable points that we were pleased to include in the final proof, and for contributing the Foreword.

We should also like to thank Howard Ridley and Rob Phillips for helping with the figures, and Marion Green for typing the manuscript.

J. J.
J. S.

Wee also have Sound-houses, where wee practise and demonstrate all Sounds, and their Generation. Wee have harmonies which you have not, of Quarter Sounds, and lesser Slides of Sounds.

Diverse instruments of Musick likewise to you unknowne, some sweeter than you have; Together with Bells and Rings that are dainty and sweet. Wee represent Small Sounds as well as Great and Deepe; Likewise Great Sounds, Extenuate and Sharpe; Wee make diverse Tremblings and Warblings of Sounds, which in their Originalle are Entire. Wee represent and imitate all Articulate Sounds and Letters and the Voices and Notes of Beasts and Birds. Wee have certain Helps, which sett to the Eare doe further the Hearing greatly. Wee also have Strange and Artificial Echoe's, reflecting the Voice many times, and as it were Tossing it; And some that give back the Voice lowder than it cam, some Shriller some Deeper; Yea some rendering the Voice, Differing in the letters or Articulate Sound, from that they receyve, Wee also have means to convey Sounds in Trunks and Pipes, in strange Lines, and Distances . . .

Francis Bacon, *The New Atlantis* (1624)

FOREWORD

All artistic media use technology of one sort or another. But music, more than any other medium, has always been dependent on 'state-of-the-art' technology for its very existence. As soon as Man understood how to process animal skins, he made drums; as soon as he learned how to cut wood, he made crude flutes. String instruments are incredibly sophisticated assemblages of diverse and exotic materials. Keyboard instruments are ingenious, fiendishly complicated machines.

The idea that some musical instruments are more 'natural' than others is pure nonsense. Except for the human voice, all musical instruments are highly contrived, wholly artificial, and utterly dependent upon the most advanced technologies of the time in which they are developed. When we view musical instruments this way, we see that the widespread use of electronics in the production of the music of our time is not a break with tradition, but a clear continuation of it.

Most of the music that we hear today comes to us through electronic equipment. At this point in time, electronics is a highly developed and mature technology. It is especially applicable to the production of music, since it is theoretically possible to produce any sound at all through electronics. Moreover, it is possible to impart many quasi-intelligent properties to electronic music-producing instruments. The limitations seem to exist more in the imaginations of us technicians, musicians and listeners than in the technology of electronics.

The education of today's musician is not complete if he does not have a practical understanding of electronic equipment. This book provides a splendid introduction to principles and equipment that are currently applied to music-making, and it does so in simple, clear, musically oriented language. The more musicians and technicians learn one another's vocabularies and thought processes, the more successfully will we be able to bring together the technology and music of our time.

Robert A. Moog

NEW YORK

GLOSSARY FOR THE AMERICAN EDITION

Bass bin Speaker enclosure containing the cone-type, low-frequency driver.

Earth Ground.

Earthing Grounding.

Earth line Ground wire, low side, or negative lead of a circuit.

Earth loop Ground loop.

Live line Hot wire, high side, or positive lead of a circuit.

FET Field Effect Transistor. A special type of transistor which has a very high input impedance.

High tension (HT) In the U.S. one thinks of high tension lines as the high voltage A.C. transmission lines running through the countryside connecting generating plants to poser distribution centers (Substations). In the U.K. high tension refers to the D.C. output of a power supply that is necessary to operate electronic equipment. It is termed high tension because for vacuum tube equipment, the nominal D.C. power supply output is in the 300 to 600 volt range. Transistor equipment is nominally 25 to 50 volts D.C. In the U.S. this power supply output is often called the B+ voltage.

Mains The commercial power source, or power line. In the U.S. this is usually 110 volts, 60 hertz (cycles per second) A.C. In the U.K. normal line voltage or mains voltage is 240 volts, 50 hz A.C., a potentially more hazardous situation.

Roadie A stage hand or, more specifically, the traveling set-up person.

Screened coaxial lead Shielded cable. In U.S. shielded cable for r.f. (radio frequency) use is called co-ax cable. Such cable has less capacitance between the leads than standard shielded cable giving it better high-frequency response. However, the positive lead (center conductor) is a solid wire making the cable less flexible and subject to earlier failure than standard shielded wire which uses a stranded center conductor.

Thermionic component For all practical purposes, the electronic vacuum tube. Vacuum tubes will work only when the cathode is heated to a point where the electrons in the cathode metal have enough energy to escape their atomic/molecular bond.

Valve Electronic vacuum tube.

Valve amplifier Vacuum tube amplifier.

Venue Performing house, theater, etc. Originally, an establishment of light entertainment such as a cabaret, vaudeville house, or music hall.

ELECTRIC MUSIC

Chapter 1

SOURCES

This chapter is about the birth of the sound itself, at the instrument; and an instrument as we refer to it need bear little resemblance to anything you might find in a symphony orchestra. However bizarre the sound-producing mechanism (and what could be more bizarre than a voltage controlled oscillator, or a tuba?), the player is still responsible for the eventual musical effect. And if you must be be conversant with the subtleties of rosin and strings to play violin, then there is clearly as much reason to understand mysterious markings on your amplifier as you plug in its electric equivalent.

The first essential is an electric signal that perfectly represents the sound you are trying to make. We call this small signal the 'source'. The source may be *hybrid*, such as the pickup on a guitar or a microphone placed near a vocalist; or it may be a pure source, such as an organ or synthesiser. In either case the source feeds an amplification system consisting of an amplifier and a loudspeaker.

Many critics of electric music sincerely believe that the whole point of amplification is to make sounds louder and so annoy as many people as possible. No doubt some musicians are guilty of this. But the most important aspect – and this is where electric music really scores – is that we can change the whole property of the sound by putting the signal from the source through a *treatment* before we amplify it and convert it to sound in the loudspeaker (see fig 1). There are many treatments we can use, such as boosting the treble part of the signal, or adding reverberation, and we deal with these in Chapter 3.

Here we are concerned with sources and consider two types – hybrid and pure electronic.

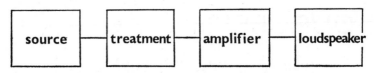

Fig 1   The basic system for electric music

HYBRID SOURCES

A hybrid source is a mixture of acoustic and electric. For example, the voice is an acoustic source, and directly produces sound energy. But these sound waves can fall on a transducer – a microphone in this case – and be converted into electrical energy. Similarly an electric guitar produces sound energy directly, although this may be small: but the vibrations of the strings can again be turned into an electric signal by means of a transducer, called a 'pickup'. We will look at some popular sources.

The electric guitar

The electric guitar can be traced back to Charlie Christian, around 1937. Originally an acoustic guitarist, wishing to be heard above the sound of five saxes, four trumpets, four trombones and so on would play into a microphone. The audience would also hear feet tapping, the musician with hiccups and the roadie walking backstage. Fastening the microphone to the body of the guitar will lose the hiccups and the roadie, and by masking the microphone with a rubber cover you should lose the phantom foot tapper. This is an improvement, but if you tap the guitar accidentally the audience will soon know.

The only sensible solution is the use of a magnetic pickup in place of the microphone. A permanent magnet is wound with a coil of many hundreds of turns of fine insulated wire, called a 'bobbin', the ends of which form the live line and the earth line, as in fig 2. There is one bobbin for each string and the whole assembly is arranged under and close to the steel strings of the guitar. If the steel string is plucked the magnetism linking the

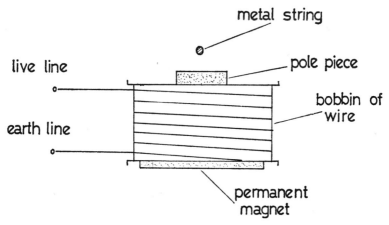

Fig 2   The magnetic pickup

bobbin of wire changes in sympathy, and a changing, or alternating, voltage is developed across the bobbin. The frequency of this voltage will be the same as the frequency of vibration of the string. This alternating voltage or signal can now be amplified perhaps 20,000 times by an amplifier and fed to a loudspeaker system, and so the volume of the guitar is boosted tremendously.

A variety of systems are used commercially, with either fixed or adjustable pole pieces, one or more pickups, and either single or twin reversed (humbucking) coils. The impedance of the combined pickup system can be low (600 to 700ohms) or high (usually 7,000 to 15,000ohms). Which is most suitable depends mainly on the input impedance of the amplifier being used. There are some very important electronic principles to establish here. Suppose the pickup is a 12,000ohm one and the amplifier is the same. When the lead from the pickup is plugged into the amplifier the signal voltage from the pickup is halved and, since power is proportional to the square of the voltage, the power output from the amplifier is a quarter of what it should be. If, however, this pickup was feeding an amp whose input impedance was 240,000ohms then you would lose only 5 per cent of the signal, not 50 per cent. The same effect would be achieved if 600ohm pickup fed the 12,000ohm amplifier. But more of this in the Appendix (see p 162).

The guitar maker has a problem here: the ideal pickup would have no resistance but as soon as he winds the bobbin he has got resistance. Increasing the number of turns on the bobbin increases its sensitivity but at the same time also increases its resistance, with consequent power loss. So a compromise has to be adopted.

Note too that the musician has got to use a screened coaxial lead from the guitar to the amplifier, particularly if the pickup is high impedance. The longer such a lead, the more is its capacitance from one wire to the other and the more the treble will be cut.

A word here about 'tone'. Many guitars now have more than one pickup. That near the bridge or fixed end of a vibrating string will pick up a lot of the higher harmonics on the string (see Appendix, p 156) and will sound harsh or trebly, while that some 6in further up the string near the finger board will sound smoother or bassy. Sometimes each pickup comes out to a separate jack socket on the guitar from which *two* leads run, one to an amp and stack on one side producing the treble sound and the other to another amp and stack on the other side producing the bass. This system is wrongly called 'stereo'. More usually, however, there is a mixing, switching and filtering circuit

14

incorporated in the body of the guitar fed by both pickups; the mixed outputs go to a single jack socket on the guitar, the tone and volume being selected by the controls on the guitar as well as on the amplifier.

A recent development here, by Dan Armstrong, is the sliding pickup, the position of which can be altered to produce an individual tone.

Finally, although the magnetic pickup overcomes all those problems of extraneous noise, it does *not* pick up all those small acoustic noises which make a guitar sound acoustically normal. Nor will it work on nylon strings. If you want these advantages you will have to go back to the contact microphone.

We have more to say about guitars in Chapter 5.

The use of bugs

A bug is an instrument transducer similar to the contact microphone of the last section, which enables a violin, piano, accordion, saxophone etc to be amplified. It also enables us to apply a treatment, such as ring modulation, to what is otherwise a genuine non-electric instrument.

A DeArmond Model 700 magnetic-type contact pickup available from Selmer is suitable for a violin, but you must be prepared to experiment. It might be necessary to fill the body of the violin with cotton wool or other deadening material such as cushion filling. The main problem with bugs is feedback direct from the loudspeaker system to the bug, which may prevent you from getting enough volume to rise above the rest of the band. You may need to change your position relative to the loudspeakers to overcome this. You might experiment with a ceramic electric bridge from Barcus and Berry in the USA, or try a Barker Sperry violin.

Bugging a piano is not easy. You can try using one or more microphones on boom stands positioned close to the strings. A great improvement is the Helpinstall piano pickup, recently invented by Charlie Helpinstall, an electronics engineer from

Houston, Texas. The device is available from Rick Wakeman's company in the UK (see Appendix, p 166). It consists of a metal bar about 4ft 6in long weighing about 10lb, fixed across the top of a grand piano. Six electromagnetic pickups suspended from it hang very close to the strings, each one individually controlled and responding to its own portion of the keyboard.

Voice and microphone

The human voice is probably the oldest 'source' known to man. A microphone, or just plain 'mike', acts as a transducer turning the acoustic energy of the voice into electric energy, which can then be treated and amplified.

A very important aspect, which could be here to stay, is the trend of groups to mike up their instruments through small amplifiers and *then* through a large PA system. More of this in Chapter 6.

There is possibly no more confusing aspect of electric music than the variety of mikes available. One maker's catalogue contains nearly thirty different types and you could collect catalogues from at least the following companies: AKG, Beyer, Calrec, Eagle, Electrovoice, Grampian, Orange, Peiker, Philips, Reslo, Sennheiser, Shure, and STC. Some makers classify their mikes by application, eg contact, lavalier, lip and radio. Others go technical and quote frequency response, sensitivity, impedance and polar response (or directional sensitivity). Some are useful for outdoors work, others we are told are of 'studio quality'. Some microphones are fairly robust; others are very delicate and can be ruined by simply blowing into them, which as every good musician knows is the best way to tell if a mike is working or not.

We will try here to guide you through the maze of technicalities so that you know you are using the right mike for the job. Basically, of course, you get what you pay for.

Carbon mike

This mike is still used in telephones but is obsolete as far as the musician is concerned. It does serve, however, as a useful introduction. Its principle is one of variation in contact resistance: the sound pressure wave alternately compresses and releases the carbon granules whose electrical resistance (see Appendix, p 163) is altered correspondingly, causing a variation in electric current. The sensitivity – the amount of voltage produced compared to the sound pressure – can only be described as 'fair', but, as with all mikes, if you halve the distance between your mouth and the mike the sound intensity will be increased four times, not twice, and you can expect four times the voltage to be generated. The frequency response – the graph of voltage produced for a given sound intensity plotted against the frequency of the sound – should be flat over the entire audio range of perceptibility (see fig 3), say from 30 cycles per second (30 hertz or 30Hz) up to 20,000 or 20 kilocycles per second (20kHz), giving a desirable wide bandwidth. The carbon mike has a limited bandwidth, making it suitable for speech only; it distorts fairly easily and is noisy.

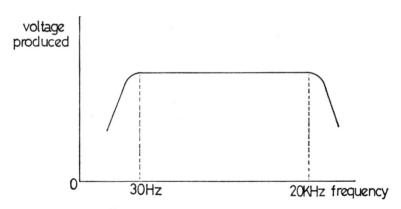

Fig 3   Ideal microphone response graph

17

Crystal (or ceramic) mike

This is the mike typically given away with a cheap tape recorder. Its principle relies on the piezo-electric effect, that certain crystals (for example, Rochelle salt) will generate a voltage when subjected to a mechanical stress from a sound wave or from the stylus in a record player.

The sensitivity is high; typically about 500mV (or 500 thousandths of a volt) can be produced when an average sound wave hits it and this could overload the sensitive inputs of modern amplifiers. Its bandwidth is quite good too, although the treble is lifted a bit, and it is very robust and cheap. One reason why it is useless to a musician is that it is omnidirectional (or polydirectional) meaning that it is sensitive all round in 360°, and will pick up sounds coming at it from all directions. We can specify this directional sensitivity of microphones by a 'polar pattern', which is a graph of the mikes' sensitivity at various angles to the incoming sound wave. A musician using a crystal mike for vocals can expect a lot of feedback.

Feedback in this sense means the sound waves coming from the loudspeakers falling on the mike and being amplified only to fall on the mike even more strongly, quickly producing that ear-shattering whistle so typical of the amateur.

Another disadvantage of the crystal mike is its very high impedance (perhaps a million ohms or 1 Megohm). This means you *must* use coaxial cable with the proper screen all around the central live wire (like a TV aerial lead), and this screen must be earthed. The snag with such a cable is that it has capacitance from the central wire to the earthed screen, which shorts out the high or treble frequencies and alters the tone, making it more bassy. The longer the lead, the worse is the effect. In practice you are limited to a length of about 5m.

Dynamic mike

Although fundamentally these important mikes are omnidirectional, they can be fitted with acoustic pads at the rear which act as a phase-changing network, transforming the polar characteristic to a heart shape or 'cardioid', so that the mike is mainly sensitive at the front only. For example, the AKG D501 can be mechanically switched between two positions, the first closing a chamber making the mike omnidirectional and suitable for outdoor work, the second opening the chamber and making the response cardioid, so that the mike is suitable for recording indoors.

The principle (fig 4A) is that the sounds fall on a diaphragm attached to a small coil of wire, which is then forced to vibrate between the poles of a magnet, generating a small voltage across the coil; hence the name 'moving coil'. The impedance is low at about 25ohms and so is the sensitivity at about 10mV. The low impedance means we can use any length of cable between the mike and the amp without loss of treble. In fact it need not even be coaxial cable, though you are less likely to pick up hum if it is. Usually a step-up transformer is incorporated within the body of the mike, which steps up both the voltage and the impedance. For choice use low impedance mikes, which will accept about 50m of cable without loss of quality, and step up at the input of the amplifier. Note that some manufacturers (AKG, Beyer, and Shure – the Shure Model 545 Unidyne 111 being a particularly good example) make dual impedance mikes and then the choice of connection is yours.

Ribbon (or velocity) mike
This is another important type particularly for studio recording work – it is a bit fragile for use on gigs. It consists of a very thin metal ribbon suspended delicately between the poles of a magnet (see fig 4B). A sound wave causes the ribbon to vibrate, generating a very small voltage across it in sympathy with the velocity of the air molecules in the sound wave. The impedance is very small, probably a fraction of an ohm, and likewise the sensitivity. A transformer is therefore usually built in to step

19

up the impedance to about 30ohms and give a sensitivity of about 3mV.

In principle the polar response is bi-directional, a 'figure of eight', the mike equally sensitive to sound waves from both front

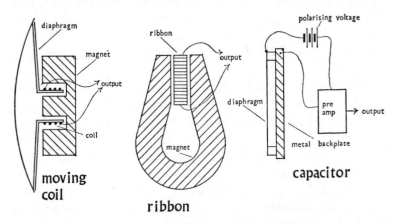

Fig 4   Dynamic, ribbon, and capacitor microphones

and rear and quite unresponsive to sounds from the sides. However, the manufacturer usually encloses the rear of the mike in an acoustic cavity, all within the casing, and this makes it quite uni-directional.

Condenser (or capacitor) mike

This is our last category: the condenser mike has emerged recently, after many improvements, as a high quality studio recording mike.

It is usually pressure-operated with a diaphragm forming one plate open to the air while the other plate is fixed at the back (see fig 4C). These two plates form an electrical capacitor, known here as a 'capsule', and this requires a polarising voltage.

Usually a 5m multi-core cable connects the mike to its special power unit, which is generally mains operated. The vibration of the diaphragm causes a change in the capacitance of the capsule and a consequent voltage change across it, due to the change in current through a large load resistor.

The sensitivity is low, about 5mV, but the bandwidth and quality are very good. Low sensitivity is immaterial provided the basic signal is of high quality, since it can always be amplified to a usable voltage. (There is no point in further amplification if the signal is bad to start with.) The impedance is basically extremely high, but is reduced usually by an FET source follower pre-amp incorporated in the body of the mike, as in the AKG.

The polar response is fundamentally omnidirectional, but modification of the polarisation voltage can change the response from omni- to bidirectional or cardioid. One manufacturer offers nine different responses, all obtained by switching the polarising supply voltage.

Frequently, and particularly in studio work where high quality and low hum levels are essential, 'balanced line' operation is preferred. But more of this in Chapter 6.

Mike Stands

A mike stand does more than loosely hold the mike in vaguely the right position. Mikes are expensive things and the collapse of a cheap stand may mean a new mike.

A good stand will protect your mike and if adjusted properly will improve your performance by placing the mike exactly where you need it, whether it is a normal straight stand for normal use or a boom stand over a keyboard or Leslie. A decent stand will have decent rubber feet on it, so helping to reduce feedback from the stage floor.

It is best to avoid stands with non-standard screws (in case you lose one) and detachable legs (for the same reason). Make sure that when it is up it stays up!

Mike technique

The musician's main enemy is feedback. To reduce the danger of

21

this to a minimum you must obviously use a good unidirectional mike, preferably a super- or hyperdirectional one, and keep the loudspeaker as near as possible to the sides of the stage. What we are really saying is that the two polar loops of the mike and loudspeaker must not overlap. As a rule you should aim to keep the mike between you and the speaker. If it still feeds back you will just have to take some of the presence or treble off at the amplifier, or reduce the volume.

Your effectiveness in projecting to the audience will be increased by bearing these points in mind:

(a) A mike is an instrument and you need to practise *with the mike*.

(b) Remember the distance from the mouth to the mike is all important; do not change it needlessly, since it will drastically change the volume the audience hears.

(c) Keep the right distance from the mike for the particular effect you want. For a harsh sound, sing louder, and back away from the mike so that you do not overdrive the input stage of the amplifier into distortion. When you want a quieter, more intimate tonal quality, sing quieter and move nearer. Do not be afraid to experiment – try coming in at the mike from the side, for example.

(d) If the equipment and the audience suffer when you say 'B', 'D', or 'P' or any other syllable that is a blast of air, you can use a pop filter – a foam or foam and wire bag that goes over the front of the mike. Of course, no material is 100 per cent acoustically transparent, and the filter will take some of the treble off too. Some mikes have such a filter built in, which you would have to remove if you were instrument miking. A small side benefit of the pop filter is that it cuts down the amount of saliva you inevitably spit into your mike, which is slowly rusting it up.

Taking care of mikes

A mike is an expensive and delicate device that should be treated with great care. On stage, do not drop it or knock the stand over; do not blow into it; do not hit it; if you want to know whether or not it is working, a discreet tap on the side will do.

When you leave the stage, wrap each mike carefully in a piece of foam rubber and place them all together tightly in a solid metal box, so that they will not be crushed in the back of the van when the load shifts. The same holds for leads too.

For best results mikes should be kept clean: you can take the metal protection cage off periodically and boil it in water.

We will finish this section with a lovely quote from the WEM catalogue – 'Feedback, and somebody spending a long time in front of an audience with each mike calling "one, two three . . . TESTING" – two of the most unprofessional sounds you'll hear.'

PURE ELECTRONIC SOURCES

A pure electronic source is just that: a box of electronics, powered by battery or mains, producing an electric signal which, if amplified, can be turned into a sound wave by means of a loudspeaker system. It bears no physical resemblance whatsoever to a conventional musical instrument.

Historical

The development of electronics this century, first with valves, later with transistors and just recently with integrated circuits, has had a considerable effect on music. Not only can we make a natural sound from an instrument louder by using an amplifier, we can also apply a treatment to the transduced sound and so alter its tone that it no longer sounds like the instrument. We can go further: we can dispense with the instrument altogether and replace it by a pure electronic source. The story does not even end there: the pure electronic source need not be played by a musician or electronics technician – a computer can play it, as we shall see later.

Early research into electronic music was done at Cologne with the Trautonium, a voltage-controlled sawtooth oscillator system with facilities for gliding tones. Another device was the Theremin which used two radio (very high) frequency oscillators: when a hand was brought near, the resulting extra capacitance changed one of the frequencies and the resulting beat frequency – the difference between the two frequencies – became audible, the pitch depending on the position of the hand, so that the device could be 'played'.

Tone generators (audio frequency oscillators)
Tone generators are electronic boxes which generate an alternating voltage of a few volts with a frequency which can be varied over the audio range, say 20Hz to 20,000Hz. Most are powered from the mains – one exception being the battery-powered Nombrex Model 40. Various shapes of waves – and therefore tones – can be obtained, the most common being sine shape (smooth flute-type tone) or square shape (buzzy sax-type tone). The output impedance is usually high, meaning it must feed a high input impedance amplifier: it could not drive a loudspeaker direct. (An exception is the Advance J2.) An engineer might call these boxes 'audio frequency oscillators' (AFO) or 'signal generators'. Basically they are precision pieces of test gear; the output control will be calibrated in volts (or mV), the frequency will be known from a scale and the sine shape quite free from distortion. You get what you pay for.

A musician may not need such great accuracy. The economical Halo 'Banshee' is not calibrated, and forms a good example of a tone generator economically produced for musicians. The two outputs, each of which can be swept in frequency (or pitch) over a large part of the audible band, are adjustable in output (or volume). One output is a sine shape and the other a ramp or triangular shape, a position being available where one oscillator locks onto the other and the device generates 'random scales' (see plate p 119).

A recent development in oscillators – and one which is certainly of great importance in synthesisers, as we shall see – is the use of 'voltage control'. Such an oscillator is called a 'voltage controlled oscillator' (VCO). In a conventional oscillator, perhaps based on a Wien Bridge circuit as is the Nombrex Model 40, the frequency is controlled by varying the resistance of part of an electronic circuit by turning a knob by hand, just as one tunes a radio. In a VCO the frequency is controlled by varying the DC voltage applied to a certain part of an electronic circuit. This too can be done manually, of course, but it can also be done entirely by electrical means called the 'control voltage'. Voltage control can be usefully applied not only to oscillators but also to filters and amplifiers, as we shall see on p 129. We shall just note here that a voltage controlled instrument has one or more operating parameters determined by the magnitude of an applied control voltage rather than by the manual setting of the panel controls.

Fig 5 shows the famous Moog VCO circuit in block diagram form. The frequency of the AC voltage produced at the output depends on the value of the DC voltage applied to the control input of the adder. Suppose a one-volt increase is applied to a control input, causing the frequency of the output to double, ie to rise by one octave. Then, since there are 12 semitones in the octave on the equal temperament scale, a control voltage rise by 1/12 volt will cause the output frequency to rise by 1 semitone.

A new breed of tone generators is rapidly becoming popular. These, quite often voltage controlled, are called 'function generators' because at the output they give various shaped waves, sine, square, sawtooth, triangular and pulse shapes, each of which has its own particular tone because of the combination of harmonics within the wave. Many contain an extra low frequency sawtooth oscillator which acts as a control voltage on the main oscillator, sweeping the frequency over a section of the audio band. The plate on p 101 shows a typical example from the USA, the Exact Electronics Model 126.

The last of our examples of pure electronic tone generators

is the Stylophone. The circuit is completed, and a sound produced, when the pen is pressed down on a key. The range is chromatic over $1\frac{1}{2}$ octaves and vibrato can be switched in.

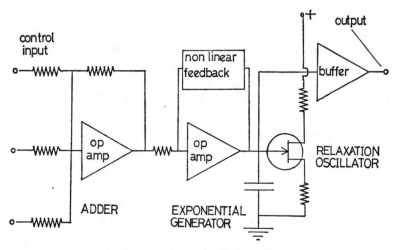

Fig 5   Voltage controlled oscillator

A low level output jack enables the signal to be amplified by an external amplifier and loudspeaker system if necessary. The tone wheel system in some Hammond organs is really electro-mechanical rather than pure electronic.

Organs
This really is an enormous field. A single company may produce several dozen types, from small portable single manual organs costing perhaps a hundred pounds or so to large console triple manual organs costing thousands of pounds. Again, you get what you pay for.

Any organ works from a keyboard but it is not alone in this. There is a tendency now to 'play keyboard', which could include organ, ordinary or acoustic piano, electric keyboard, mellotron and synthesiser. A top class keyboard man like Rick Wakeman in

26

the UK could well be surrounded on stage by £20,000 worth of gear.

The rise of the organ has been nothing short of dramatic. The trade is experiencing a boom; about 70 per cent of electric organs sold go into ordinary homes, although only 10 per cent of the purchasers have any musical skill. Consequently, and quite reasonably, the manufacturers produce organs which match the sideboard, contain artificial drummers, incorporate cassette tape recorders, and have a headphone facility for silent practice so that Fred will not disturb Mabel watching the TV.

The electric organ has come a long way from the 1930s, when the Mighty Wurlitzer rose from the pit of the local cinema. The Wurlitzer was viewed with awe by a world surrounded by acoustic instruments; it was very loud and had a variety of special sound effects at the touch of a tab. But it was more akin to the old hand-pumped organ and its delayed action mechanics made it quite unsuitable for music involving brisk syncopation.

The electric organ had no pipes and so was no longer a fixture in the building – like central heating – and could be used by our wandering gig musician. Milt Herth, Fela Sowande, and Milt Buckner – the pianist with Lionel Hampton – were among the first exponents in the USA. Some time later Jimmy Smith gave the Hammond organ its first true jazz sound, such recordings as 'Walk on the Wild Side' having a tremendous international influence.

Fig 6 shows a block diagram of a typical organ system. Initially an electric signal has to be generated. Basically there are two ways to do this. One way is the 'tone wheel' system, now associated with the older Hammond models. A toothed wheel made of a ferromagnetic material rotates close to a coil and magnet assembly, and every time a tooth passes by a small voltage is induced in the coil. If 440 teeth pass every second then 440 electric voltage pulses are induced in the coil every second, producing a note of 440Hz. Wheels with different numbers of teeth produce different notes and the whole assembly

27

can run from one motor, the speed of which must be constant or the whole organ will drift out of tune. It is the attainment of this constant speed which gives some Hammonds a complex starting up procedure. There can be as many as ninety tone wheels and they generate not only the fundamentals but the harmonics as well (see Appendix, p 156). The only Hammonds still produced in 1974 which incorporate tone wheels are the models A100, C3 and T500.

The Hammond Concorde, which features harmonic tone bars, has the sound of tone wheels but achieves this by the use of pure electronic large-scale integrated circuits (LSIs).

The alternative to this electro-mechanical method of tone generation is the pure electronic way, and most manufacturers are now taking advantage of the latest electronic discoveries to produce solid state organs. These can consist of discrete components such as transistors, resistors, and capacitors all separately soldered together into modules, or – more recently – the use of integrated circuits. In both cases the volume of space necessary for the electronics within the organ is less, leaving room for other circuitry such as automatic rhythm. Such organs are also much more reliable. The electronic circuits used to generate the signal are similar to tone generators (see p 24), the only essential difference being that here the circuits must be extremely stable and produce precisely the same frequency for any length of time under varying conditions of temperature and humidity, even when the mains voltage varies. This is not easy but it can be achieved.

A two-manual organ with pedals might have forty-four notes in each of the manuals and thirteen in the pedals, making 101 different notes. You might expect the electronics engineer to have a field day and use 101 different tone generator circuits, but he knows there are only twelve semitones in the octave. So he uses only twelve-tone generators and obtains the other notes by electronic 'dividers'; a computer circuit called an 'Eccles-Jordan' is often used. For example, one tone generator (the 'A') may be tuned to oscillate at precisely 14,080Hz. This is fed to the first divider, which turns it into a note an octave lower, 7,040Hz. This then feeds the second divider to produce 3,520Hz and so on down the octaves producing 1,760, 880, 440, 220, 110, 55 and $27\frac{1}{2}$Hz.

The $27\frac{1}{2}$ and 55Hz signals are then available to the pedal keys (see fig 6) as 'A' bass notes, and the 220Hz might be available as an 'A' on the lower manual and the 440Hz as an 'A' at about the same hand position on the upper manual. But the harmonics are available too. On the upper manual the 880Hz is available as the second harmonic, the 1,760Hz as the third, the 3,520Hz as the fourth, the 7,040Hz as the fifth and so on. On some organs the 440Hz would be called 16ft, the 880Hz is then 8ft, and so on, a system based on the pipe organ. On some organs definite amounts of these harmonics are mixed in the voicing circuit and brought in by tabs marked 'oboe', 'trumpet', and so on. On the other hand some organs leave the harmonics available at drawbars, one for each harmonic, and the amount which each harmonic contributes to the overall sound is determined by the player and not the manufacturer. Some manufacturers incorporate *both* systems (see plate p 101).

Other facilities are usually available as well. Vibrato can be switched in or out on either manual, and sustain can perhaps be added to the bass notes. The whole sound can be given reverberation and expression can be applied by changing the overall intensity of sound using a swell pedal. Percussion facilities may be available, governing the envelope of the sound produced and are essential for a funky sound. Automatic rhythm may be available (and some varieties actually keep time with you) and a rotary speaker system added. For more on these refinements see Chapter 3.

More recent developments include the addition of cassette recorders and small synthesisers.

Most of the large manufacturers, like Hammond, Lowrey, and Thomas, also include a variety of special circuits to give special

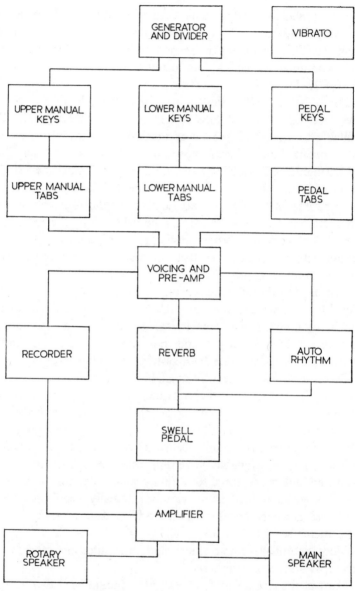

Fig 6   Electronic organ system

effects. Such words as Autochord, automatic organ computer, Golden Harp, Brass Symphoniser, Stereo and so on are used with abandon. Clever though such circuits are, they add to the cost and probably appeal more to Fred than to our budding superstar.

Finally, a word on amplification. If the organ contains an amplifier you can safely assume that it is rated to take the organ safely and not blow the loudspeaker or distort badly. However, if you are travelling and using a portable organ like the Vox Continental 300 – and you could do far worse – the choice of an amplifier is yours. In our opinion it is no good trying 15W or 15W combination amps or you will sound like Sooty. You need plenty of capacity to cope with chords on the lower manual and large speakers to cope with the bass. A 50W combo amp with two 12in speakers might cope, but even bigger would be better. We find the 70W Hammond Leslie 825 ideal. If more volume is needed we can always 'mike up' (see Chapter 5, p 95).

Electric pianos
Unlike the organ, the use of an electric piano is a fairly recent development. Ray Charles used it on 'What'd I Say' back in 1959 in the USA. The electric piano produces a rich, chunky, percussive sound that has added a whole new dimension to sound in the last decade or so. All instruments are portable and prices range from the Sound City Jo'anna at less than £200 to the Fender Rhodes at over £800. The plate on p 102 shows the former.

The Pianomate by Dubreq in the UK is an ingenious device that electrifies any piano. The plate on p 102 shows the arrangement. It consists of two double-octave units whose contacts move with the piano keys to augment the natural piano sound with organ-type tone colours. A foot volume control, two-speed vibrato and three-position tone control are provided, as is the facility to change the pitch of the device by as much as a semitone to bring it into line with the typical gig piano.

Mellotron

Synthetic tone colours from any organ, no matter how good, can sound boring to listen to after a while, although the use of vibrato, Leslies, and good musicianship all help to delay the onset of this dreaded problem. The Mellotron should not be guilty of this because it uses pre-recorded tapes of actual instruments. First available in 1963 in a complex and expensive

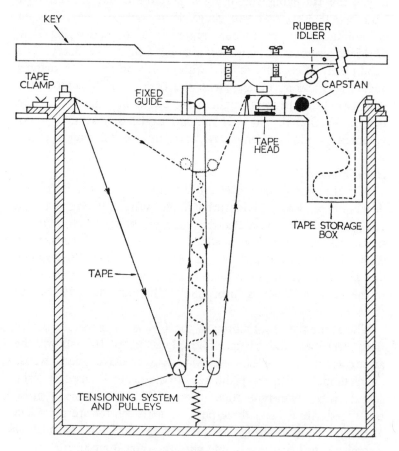

Fig 7   Mellotron 400 tape transport system

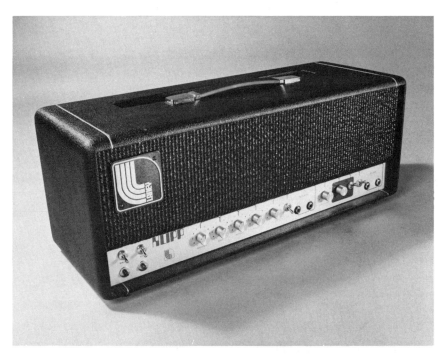

Page 33 (*above*) Laney KLIPP Guitar Amplifier. This standard-style valve amp features a signal-clipping device to increase sustain at any volume level; (*below*) WEM Slave Amplifier: This is a power stage only, driving its own speaker cabinets, and is used to increase the total output of a standard amplifier

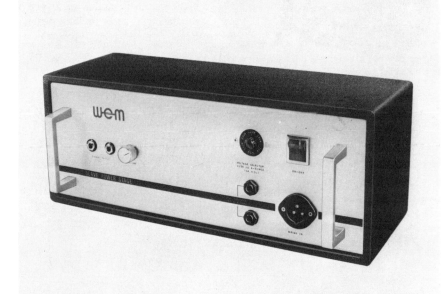

Page 34 (*left*) WEM Vendetta PA Column. The speaker cloth has been removed to show the three pairs of drive units – bass, mid-range, and horns (for the treble); (*below*) Millbank Musicmaster Mixer. This has eight channels, and is of a type increasingly used in large-scale PAs

form, a smaller, cheaper version is now available, the Mellotron 400. This version contains the sounds of flute, violin and cello and is played like any keyboard. Fig 7 shows the tape transport system used. When the key is pressed down the rubber idler engages with the capstan, pulling tape into the tape storage box. The tape is kept in tension by the plastic pulleys and tension spring. When the key is released the tension spring contracts, pulling the tape back out of the tape storage box.

There is one three-track tape for each of the thirty-five keys on the keyboard, and the track selector enables you to choose any of these. If you choose 'flute sound' and press one key down, you get the sustained sound of one flute. If you then play a four-note chord, say, you get the sound of four flutes playing in harmony. Other tapes can of course be included in the Mellotron.

The synthesiser

The latest development in keyboard music, and perhaps the most exciting one, is the synthesiser, a pure electronic device that enables a competent user (with a lot of patience, time and a tape recorder) to synthesise or build up the sound of a musical instrument from its individual harmonics. A keyboard as such is not essential.

Synthesisers have been around since the 1950s at least, but they were thermionic and consequently large. The development of transistors and their associated circuitry, and more recently integrated circuits, coupled with Bob Moog's ideas on voltage control about 1965, led to the suitcase size synthesiser of which the EMS Synthi-A, shown in plate on p 120, is an example.

Synthesisers are dealt with at length in Chapter 7.

Chapter 2

AMPLIFIERS AND LOUDSPEAKERS

The advent of electrical energy as a convenient and universal source of power in the early years of the present century did not at first have any real application in the field of music; apart from perhaps removing a serious fire hazard to the pianist, who no longer needed candles to feebly illumine his music. The development of radio and its associated amplification of very small signals into audible form were more directly relevant to music as such; given the valve amplifier in its developed state, it was only a small step to realise that a musical instrument could be made to produce louder sounds than originally intended, via an appropriate transducer.

Classical music had no real need for any such devices, of course; it was not until Stockhausen moved into electronic production of sound that 'straight' music could be said to have taken any notice at all of the new techniques available to it. It was the booming growth of dance music, and particularly American jazz, in the 1920s and 1930s which provided the ideal area for experiment of this type; and these musicians, with no rules to follow save their own, had few inhibitions toward new ideas. Jazz, with its associated dance music (the two were at first inseparable), was loud, brash and exciting; it demanded a high level of volume to achieve its less cerebral ends. Thus the bands contained large numbers of players, including sections of trumpets and saxophones voiced to carry the melody en masse, and percussion was heavily prominent in a way unknown before; solo passages had of necessity to be given to instruments with enough natural volume to carry above the rest of the band, trumpets and alto saxophones being most suited. The first problem occurred with vocalists: few of them had had any training in old style voice production, and they found it difficult to rise above the band volume or to fill larger halls. In radio and recording studios microphones were now common enough; it was an obvious step to introduce microphones on-stage to amplify the vocalist, bandleaders' announcements, and solo passages from the quieter wind instruments, through an embryo public address system. This system would be a fixture, and was of course found only in the larger and more important venues. We are now, historically, at about 1939–40.

It was the jazz and blues guitarists of this period who were responsible for initiating the next major advance. The guitar was an important instrument in Black American culture; the folk-instrument of all the early blues players, it had suffered a decline with the growth of the large jazz band, mainly because it could no longer be heard. It was relegated to the role of a rhythmic chord machine, less important than the piano or drums, and with the long sinuous melodies of the blues players forgotten. It became a standing joke that the first man to be fired in the band was the guitar player. In the early 1940s, moved by frustration at this state of affairs, two guitarists in widely different areas of music created a workable means of amplification for the instrument; small magnets, each wound with fine wire, were clipped under the strings, the tiny electrical voltages thus induced being fed to the amplifier and loudspeaker of a radio set. The electric guitar was now placed dynamically on a level with the brass and percussion, and a musical revolution was to follow quickly.

37

Once the principle of this simple magnetic transducer had been fully grasped, progress was rapid; any stringed instrument could be amplified by this means, and by the late 1940s electric guitars and amplifiers were much as we know them today, prominent in this advance being the firms of Gibson and Fender, both American. Economic considerations ended the big bands, and small groups of four to five players gained the ascendancy, their instruments directly or indirectly amplified to give levels of volume as great as a large number of acoustic players. The emphasis, however, was still on the amplification of the original acoustic sound, and it was not until the blues, in its revitalised guise of rhythm and blues and rock music, toppled jazz in the mid and late fifties that the full potential of electric instruments was gradually realised.

This new music, its performers and the booming youth culture that mushroomed with it, had even less regard for tradition than the jazzmen that they replaced; and soon electric instruments achieved a stature of their own, producing sounds and tonal effects impossible with, and unrelated to, acoustic instruments of any kind. The amplifier was now part of the instrument in its own right, and the manipulation of electronics has become a required area of instrumental technique. Whereas the early players had perforce to play the best they could with the instruments available to them from an alien culture, electronics enabled rock musicians to develop their own tools, suited to a new method of sound generation.

In the preceding chapter we discussed the tonal sources at present available for amplification to usable levels in a musical context; more will doubtless be developed as performers discover a need for the expression of new ideas. Now we must fully comprehend the function of the amplifying system as such. The electric instrument, of whatever variety, feeds a very tiny electric voltage to the amplifier (often only a few millivolts); this must be made more powerful by the amplifier, until it is sufficient to drive a loudspeaker (about 20 to 30V). This enlargement of the original signal should ideally be accompanied by no additions to, or distortions of, the original waveform. The loudspeaker is in essence a simple transducer, the electrical energy provided by the amplifier moving a diaphragm, which in turn creates a disturbance of the air mass in front of it, and produces audible sound waves (see fig 8). The loudspeaker replaces the body, horn or soundbox of a conventional instrument as the sound-producing medium.

It will be readily appreciated that the quality of the emergent

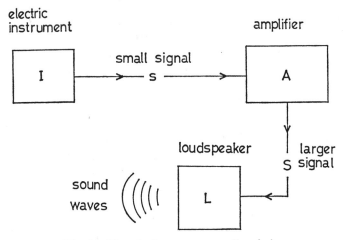

Fig 8   Electric instrument audio chain

sound is dependent on many factors; a musical sound is often an extremely complex waveform, with numerous harmonics and subtleties of tonal content (see Appendix, p 150). Any failure of any of the electronic links in our audio chain to translate exactly these nuances to the air will result in the degradation of the musical sound. Quality must therefore be a prime factor in our consideration and use of electronic equipment, and quality (as in all previous musical instruments) means expense. Almost all sound amplification is operated by mains voltage, and this is of course lethal if applied direct to the human body; it is therefore essential to observe correct procedure with regard to the wiring and earthing of such equipment, particularly when it is subjected to prolonged and arduous use in a professional situation. Advice should be obtained from a qualified electrician, and we have included some general hints on the use of mains equipment in Chapter 4. We will now look at the available equipment in the light of its suitability for specific applications.

INSTRUMENT AMPLIFIERS

In fig 9 we have a schematic layout of the basic instrument amplifier; the controls and major components are common to any make and type of amplifier, differing in detail and sophistication only. These components will be contained in a substantial

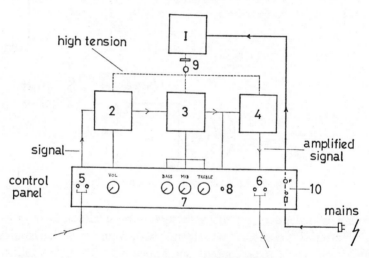

Fig 9   Basic amplifier layout

KEY
1: power supply unit (with transformer)
2: pre-amp
3: filters
4: power amp
5: input from instrument
6: outputs to speakers
7: tone filters
8: slave output
9: standby & HT fuse
10: mains on/off, neon and fuse

wooden case, and embellished with whatever stylistic fancy is currently fashionable, to produce the familiar band amp (see plate p 35). The line from the instrument is connected to one of the input sockets, the performer then having control over the sound produced via the rotary (or slide) potentiometers on the front panel. The basic controls affect loudness (on the volume control) and the tone of the sound via filters which can boost or cut bass and treble frequencies from the overall signal. Some amplifiers give control over the middle frequencies also. A recent development has been to give the operator much greater control over his tone selection by the use of many more filters, each controlling only a very narrow portion of the sound spectrum; by this means the instrumentalist has far greater choice of tone colour, but the facility is at present available on only one range of amplifiers (Dan Armstrong).

It is not proposed to include in these pages a catalogue of the various manufacturers' products, nor to make specific recommendations as to individual items of equipment. The reader must make up his own mind what to buy; our task must be to simplify his choice by clarifying the function and suitability of equipment generally. In the final analysis, the purchase of a piece of sound equipment must always be a subjective matter, based simply on what sounds good to the performer; paper specifications mean little in so highly emotive an area as playing music. Any worthwhile retailer of amplification and associated equipment should have proper facilities for the trial and evaluation of the goods he is selling, preferably at a volume level near to that at which it will eventually be used. After all, large sums of money are involved; and mistaken purchases have an untoward habit of becoming suddenly valueless on trade-in or attempted resale. It is well worth sticking to the better known manufacturers: quality combination amps also tend to hold their value well.

All instrument amplifiers will broadly follow our outlined specification; the main point being that some will perform rather better than others, or just differently. The choice of equipment can conveniently be summed up via the following considerations: WHAT FOR (ie what instrument), WHAT POWER, and HOW MUCH (ie cost). Almost any electric instrument can be fed successfully into the standard amplifier, provided the amp has a flat and fairly broad frequency response. Some manufacturers, however, design their amps for specific applications, such as bass, lead, or organ, and these will have a response curve and tonal range suited to that instrument; it is obviously necessary to determine this point beforehand. Speakers, of course, are a different animal, and must be matched to the source being amplified.

Power ratings are often confusing or misleading. No single amps are generally available more powerful than 200W, and the most common output powers available are 50W and 100W; the confusion arises because different makers use different ways of measuring and expressing the power rating of their products, via watts RMS, peak, music power, etc. These are all fairly meaningless terms in the context of the eventual loudness of the sound, which depends on so many other factors; it is best to base your comparisons only on RMS watts ratings. Twice the output power does *not* mean twice as loud. Even RMS ratings can be misleading in that the power output can vary according to the load being driven; a given amplifier may produce 100W RMS into an 8ohm load, 85W into 16ohms, but around 120W into 4ohms. It will be appreciated that the use of the lowest impedance speakers available (provided that the amplifier is designed to drive them and has output tappings for that purpose) can give a useful increase in realisable output.

The usual way of increasing output power beyond about 200W is to incorporate slave amplifiers into the set-up. These have no mixing or pre-amp stages, and consist merely of a power amplifier with speaker outputs, coupled to a low-level output from the main amp and driving additional speaker enclosures (see plate on p 33). As many slave amps as desired can be coupled up, to realise very high outputs; this technique is widely used in large-scale public address systems.

If an amplifier is driven beyond its rated output, DISTORTION or clipping of the waveform will result. Until recently this effect was regarded as undesirable, the sound being a degraded or altered version of the original signal, such as manufacturers are in general at pains to avoid. New music has demanded new techniques, however, and guitarists discovered that this type of distortion could be very useful to them by increasing the decay time or sustain of individual notes. This principle will

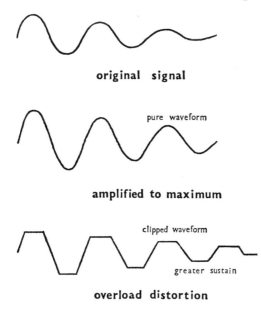

original signal

pure waveform

amplified to maximum

clipped waveform

greater sustain

overload distortion

Fig 10   Increase of sustain by signal clipping

be readily appreciated on studying fig 10; the use of this additional sustain means that full volume must be applied to the amplifier and the effect cannot be produced at low levels. It has become so widely used however, being an integral part of many great instrumentalists' technique, that some amplifiers now incorporate a switchable circuit to produce this effect at any level of volume.

All amplifiers at first used valve or thermionic components; solid state or transistor designs have by now completely replaced valves in the hi-fi field, and have roughly a half share in band amplification. The advantages of solid state circuitry include greater efficiency in the conversion of power, less heat to be dissipated, a reduction in weight, longer life of major components, and the easier incorporation of circuit protection devices into the design. For all practical purposes there need be no difference in the quality of the sound produced as compared with the very best valve designs. Lead guitarists still favour valve amps because their characteristic type of overload distortion is in general a more acceptable sound, clipping of the peaks being less sharply defined. Another advantage of valves is their plug-in fitting, which makes replacement a straightforward and unskilled proposition, though the valve's shorter service life may largely outweigh this apparent advantage. It is this author's personal opinion that a good valve amp has a certain presence and life lacking from the guitarist's point of view in solid state equivalents; this quality has nothing to do with paper specifications, but is rather in the realm of subjective impression. For applications of slaving, mixing and straightforward power amplification, the transistor is beyond doubt better.

Additional to our outline specification are various features, many of which will be included as a matter of course. Essential these days are the following:

Slave outputs have already been mentioned, and present the correct signal level to additional slave amplifiers, which can be used to augment the original power output. *Fuses*, for both mains and high-tension circuits, should be of the cartridge type and readily accessible without dismantling the amplifier. *Open circuit* and *overload* (or *short circuit*) protection should be built in to all solid state amps.

Items which vary in their degree of desirability according to

44

the intended use of the amp, and which will not be found on many manufacturer's more basic products, are as follows:

Treble boost, which provides extra lift to the top frequencies beyond that available on the treble filter. This is useful in the main only to guitarists, who may find additional treble indispensable in certain acoustic conditions, or to achieve a particular sound. *Presence* is another additional filter, designed to lift treble only, or on some amplifiers both ends of the sound spectrum. *Reverb,* when incorporated into the amplifier, is usually of the Hammond spring-type, giving a variable depth of reverberation – not an echo effect, be it noted, as reverb contains an infinite number of reflections of the original sound (see Chapter 3, p 67). *Standby* circuits enable the mains circuit to be switched on independently of the high-tension current on valve amps, allowing the amp to be idled when not in use (between sets) but ready for instant use when required. Output *Ohmage selectors* allow a choice of speaker cabinets with differing impedances. They will normally have settings for 16, 8, and 4ohms; a useful power increase can be obtained if the lowest impedance speakers are used. Lastly, a few instrument amps are equipped with a signal level meter of the VU (volume unit) type, which enables the player to monitor his output for power level or distortion; this item is frankly a bit of a luxury but can be useful to dispel (or confirm) worries about your amp's performance in rooms with bad acoustics. On PA mixers and amps, of course, it is a very desirable feature.

PUBLIC ADDRESS AMPLIFIERS

PA amplifiers have only one additional distinction; they must accept a number of incoming signals rather than one, and combine them into a balanced output; otherwise they are of essentially similar construction to the instrument amplifier. It is necessary to expand the pre-amp/mixer stage, increasing the number of inputs available and multiplying the gain stages correspondingly; and there we have a potted description of the standard PA amp. In appearance, we have a box as before, but with additional input sockets and rotary or linear controls, and with at least two speaker outlets. These basic amps are usually matched with a pair of column speakers, which are placed on each side of the stage in order to spread the sound, and the total power available will be in the region of 50 to 200W: up to about four channels is usual. Great, we think, problem solved, doesn't cost any more than a guitar amp and speakers, plug the mikes in, the piano in, flute, saxes and Charlie's bass drum and away we go. But on consideration, it will readily be appreciated that we may be expecting rather a lot from such a set-up.

If by the term PA system we mean anything other than direct instrument amplification, and are including not merely vocals (which are difficult enough in themselves) but acoustic instruments of all sorts, then our system will have to be a great deal more sophisticated if there is to be any chance of success. Acoustic instruments have a very varied range of frequency and tonal characteristics (see p 150), from the low peaking transients of a large drum to the highest upper partials of a violin note. The human voice itself has a wider range than is generally recognised, being particularly rich in harmonic content. Our PA amplifier is thus faced with a far more demanding task than a single instrument amp, which may be tailor-made to one specific purpose; and so the standard amp, which merely has a few extra inputs, is really only suitable for simple vocal application, involving around three to four vocal mikes of balanced characteristics. The answer to our problem is provided by a more serious consideration of the MIXER stage.

The greatest single problem with simple PA amps is their lack of flexibility in the control over individual tone and volume levels for each mike necessary to achieve a balanced sound devoid of feedback. In fig 11 we have clarified the function of a more advanced mixer circuit, which should ideally add no noise or distortion of its own to the single (or double for stereo) output. Each input channel now has its own volume and tone filters, providing a flexible control over any audio signals, no matter how diverse; if we couple a mixer such as this to a power amp of flat response over the widest range likely to be encountered, the result will be an amp such as the WEM Reverbmaster. This combined mixer/power amp has in addition facilities for stage monitor control, stereo operation, and slave amp outputs and built-in reverberation is available on all channels; the nominal power of 100W RMS is easily increased by slaving.

The next step in the evolution of the PA system involves

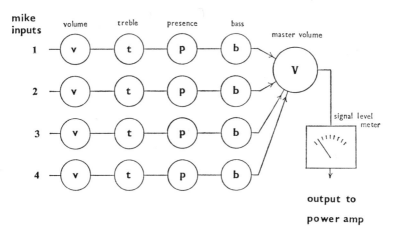

Fig 11   PA amplifier mixer function

the physical separation of the mixer and the power amplifier(s) into distinct entities, each adaptable to specific situations. The PA amp has now become an all-embracing system of band amplification, and the mixer will be enlarged to the point where it is under the control of a sound engineer (see Chapter 4, p 82). Mixers like the one illustrated in plate on p 34 can accept large numbers of mike inputs, and will feed amplifiers operating in multiple to achieve any desired power output. So perhaps the very term PA amp has now become obsolescent, and we must now consider only mixers and power stages for serious audio work; the ordinary PA amp was at best a rather dubious compromise.

SPEAKER SYSTEMS

So far, so good; we have a large pile of black boxes but nothing for them to drive. So we must next take a look at loudspeakers, perhaps the most imponderable link in the audio chain. Whereas we can arrive at an amplifier which distorts almost not at all, neglects none of our worthy frequencies, and allows us to obtain any tone from Charlie Christian to Hendrix, the loudspeaker we expect to deliver the final product is a much less sophisticated thing. To understand why, let us start with a few diagrams. In fig 12 we have the basic construction of this electro-mechanical transducer. A coil of wire is free to move within the field of a large permanent magnet; the fluctuating music signal produces a varying magnetic field within the coil, and the interaction between this and the static field of the permanent magnet results in a piston-like movement of the coil. Attached to one end of the coil is a cone, usually made of a light stiff material such as thick paper, or nowadays some plastics material; as the coil moves, so must the cone, and so in turn the air surrounding it.

From this short description it will be readily understood that a single speaker is likely to have a hard time dealing with a complex music signal. Low frequencies will produce large excursions of the cone, and will demand a large speaker to move the surrounding air in sympathy; the magnet must be massive to prevent 'ringing' on sharp transients, but the cone surround must be flexible enough to allow rapid movements which do not noticeably lag behind the electrical impulse. High frequencies will be better served by a small diameter cone, allowing more rapid vibration rates. Can we expect one speaker to cope? Perhaps not. So in general, our ideal should be different speakers for different frequency ranges, an ideal which has for long been totally ignored by most basic band equipment.

It is really quite amazing that such a Heath Robinson

contraption should work as well as it does. Since no one has come up with an alternative which is as easy or cheap to manufacture, a basically unpromising device has been refined to the point of working rather well. Almost unbelievably well in

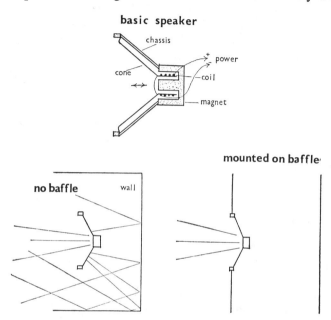

Fig 12   Loudspeaker construction

some cases; which is why we termed the whole area as imponderable; for example, that classic guitar amp, the Fender Reverb, has two speakers mounted in an open-back cabinet. Admittedly they are Lansing speakers, but their installation looks most unpromising, surrounded as they are by assorted bits of amplifier. And the sound? Fantastic.

A speaker on its own, suspended in free air, will not produce a good sound; sound radiated from the rear of the speaker will be moving in opposite phase (ie direction) from that radiated by the front, and if left free to impinge on the ear of the

49

listener will produce cancellation of the signal, resulting in a loss of volume (see Appendix, p 154). By mounting the speaker on a baffle, fig 12, in the form of a high-density board, we can prevent the rear out-of-phase components from interfering with the frontal radiation. To be effective, however, the baffle would have to be very large (up to 25ft across!), and that is not very practical. The next step is to bend the edges of the baffle round to form a box or enclosure, and give it the grand title of an 'infinite baffle system' (see fig 13): this IB type of enclosure

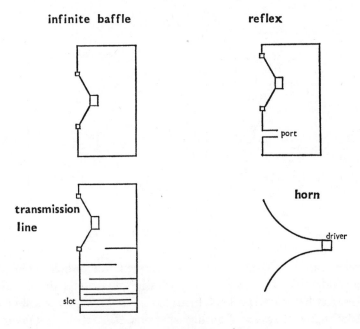

Fig 13   Loudspeaker enclosures

is the most commonly used for band speakers. The number of speakers inside the cabinet will vary, of course, as will their size; four 12in heavy-duty speakers are most common for general applications (guitar, organ, etc). Two 15in speakers will also

(*left*) SAI Bass-Bin and Horn. The bass-bin, which is in effect a folded horn, is a design which has its origin in cinema sound systems. Bands will use cabinets such as this in multiple

(*right*) TEAC Model A-3340 four-channel tape machine. This model is used extensively by small Demo Studios, and offers excellent facilities for the amateur in a home studio

Page 52 26 channel to 16 track Recording Console by Rupert Neve, installed in the studios of Pye Records Ltd, London, UK. Desks such as these offer complete flexibility of technique to the recording engineer

be found for bass or organ work, and, less often, a single 18in for bass only. In simple PA columns, which are usually also IB, 10in or 12in speakers are usual, in multiples of four: the larger speakers are intended to handle instruments producing the lowest frequencies. Power handling will be anything up to around 200W, depending on the rating of the drive units; both the power handling and the impedance of the enclosure must be matched to the output of the amplifier. It is usual to allow an excess of speaker capacity.

Simple IB cabinets such as these have a number of disadvantages. Since the speakers are of the same size in a typical band product, only a fairly narrow frequency range will be handled; the total enclosure of the speakers means that the air inside the cabinet is 'stiff', making it more difficult for the cone to move freely. As a result, lower frequencies will tend to be attenuated, and the overall efficiency of the system is low in terms of sound output for power input. For general band use, any of the reputable manufacturer's products will be satisfactory, so long as a really hi-fi sound is not expected, particularly on miked acoustic instruments.

There are two other variations on our theme of speaker in a box. A reflex enclosure is not totally sealed, but has a hole in the lower half of the cabinet. Behind this hole is a pipe of carefully calculated length, known as a 'tuned port'. Higher frequencies will not be affected, since their shorter wavelength 'traps' them within the box, but the lower notes will be phase-inverted by the length of the port, to be radiated in phase. This type of design can both extend the lower range of the cabinet and increase efficiency, since the air inside is now more flexible. A few cabinets of this type are available, mainly intended for use with bass guitar. The second variation is really a development of the reflex, and is known as the transmission line enclosure. The rear of the speaker faces into a long, gradually tapered port, folded inside the cabinet and terminating in a heavily damped slot; this extends the response of the enclosure even further, but produces disadvantages of large size and loss of efficiency. Such designs are usually found only in the hi-fi field and in studio monitor systems. To improve the frequency response of a single enclosure to the point where it is capable of handling a complex music signal, it will be necessary to use up to three different types of driver, each handling a different part of the audio range; in plate on p 34 we have illustrated an advanced PA column incorporating two 12in bass units, two 10in mid range drivers, and two horns for high frequencies. A crossover network is included to separate the frequencies and deliver them to the appropriate speaker.

Horns are a modern development of one of the earliest methods of sound reproduction, where the diaphragm or driver is acoustically linked to the surrounding air by a flared horn rather than a cone. Such a device has several advantages over the conventional speaker enclosure. It is far more efficient in terms of acoustic power or sound pressure for a given electrical input, and radiation from it is effectively confined to a very narrow angle in the frontal plane; both these factors are advantageous in a band PA system, since less amplifier power is needed to produce a given volume level, and the sound can be directed very accurately, reducing the likelihood of feedback. Let us clear away one popular misconception: the horn itself does not (or should not) vibrate, since this would introduce unwanted colouration and resonances into the sound; the horn, like the speaker enclosure, should merely couple the driver effectively to the surrounding air.

Band PA systems use the exponential type of horn, in which the flare increases as an exponent of the length; this gives a less cumbersome shape than the hyperbolic type and a wider frequency range than the conical. Treble range horns, which are usually fairly small and often segmented, can be added to ordinary IB enclosures (with a crossover) to boost higher range capacity, and it has become fairly common for manufacturers to include them as an extra on their standard PA columns. The best results will be obtained only by using a completely matched all horn set-up, and this means replacing the standard IB enclosures with bass-bins; these, developed from cinema sound techniques, consist of a large speaker as drive unit to handle low and mid frequencies, coupled to a horn. Since the horn must be very long to cope adequately with bass frequencies it is folded inside a box to produce a conveniently shaped unit (see plate p 51).

To sum up: power capacity should be about twice the output rating of the amplifier (RMS watts) to ensure a safe overload margin and smooth handling of peaks. Electric guitar can be matched with 10in or 12in units in IB enclosures, and will benefit from treble extension via tweeters or horns. Bass guitar will need 12in, 15in or (perhaps) 18in drivers, preferably in a reflex cabinet, the enclosure having a fundamental resonance well below 35Hz. Organ and other wide range instruments will need an enclosure capable of handling both bass and treble, although reasonable results can be had from four 12in IB. PA systems can use simple column speakers, but better would be columns with horn treble units, and better still an all-horn set-up. A wide-range high-power horn PA system will success-fully handle the signal from any electric or acoustic instrument.

COMBINATION AMPLIFIERS

Combination amplifiers, having mixer, power amp and speakers combined in one self-contained cabinet, represent the oldest and until recent years most widely used form of music ampli-fication. They possess all our previously mentioned features, and are at present enjoying a resurgence of popularity among guitarists. In a typical combo amp the amplifier and mixing stage occupy the top portion of the cabinet with the control panel, and two 12in speakers are mounted below. The lower part of the cabinet has space for storage of the mains lead, and in some models a reverb unit is also housed here. Output powers of most types will not exceed 50W and may be as low as 5W in small practice amps. The great advantage of a self-contained unit is its convenience, with only one box to cart about instead of two or three. However, there are also many disadvantages which led to its loss of popularity in the mid sixties. Compact cabinet dimensions impose a limitation on both the power output and the types of instrument which the unit can handle, bass guitar for instance being rather unsuited; large diameter speakers cannot easily be accommodated, and the low frequencies will subject the amplifier components to harmful vibration. High power outputs would require enlargement of the cabinet to the point of inconvenience; it is difficult to provide a well designed speaker enclosure when much of the internal space is occupied by amplifier components. For stage use, then, the separate amplifier and multiple-speaker cabinet set-up became the norm, with the combined amp used mostly in the studio or in small venues where high volume was unnecessary.

The advent of large system PAs has made very large individual amplifiers for instruments superfluous, since a low volume signal can now be miked up and fed out at balanced level through a horn PA. This technique has led to the appearance of a new generation of combination amps intended for guitarists, with the emphasis on tone quality. Most of these modern versions include in their circuitry the features mentioned on p 45, and some have the additional feature of a low-level output for the PA, making 'miking up' unnecessary. Among outstanding combination amps we should mention the Fender range, where the amount of good sound produced from one small cabinet quite baffles any attempt at explanation.

Chapter 3
TREATMENTS

In fig 1 we illustrated the basic system for electric music. Before the signal from our source is fed to the amplifier and on to the loudspeaker system we can, if we wish, subject it to a modification or *treatment*.

Now we show on pp 148–53 that as far as musicians are concerned there are five characteristics of a sound. These are:

(1) Amplitude of the signal, which governs the eventual loudness of the sound.

(2) Frequency of the signal, which determines the pitch.

(3) Harmonic content of the signal, which governs the tone.

(4) Starting transient of the signal, which also governs the tone.

(5) Envelope shaping of the signal, which determines the rate of change of loudness of the sound, and also governs the tone. If we simply feed the source direct to the amplifier all we get is the sound made louder, and possibly distorted (if we drive the amp too hard with too big a signal). This is simply the first of the five characteristics. So circuits like pre-amplifiers or mixers are not described as 'treatments'.

TREATING THE LOUDNESS

Tremolo

In the tremolo treatment the amplitude of the signal is made to increase and decrease slightly at a rate of between five and ten times a second, that is, at a frequency of between 5 and 10Hz (see fig 14). Officially it is called 'amplitude modulation' or 'AM' and, if you know about radio, you will recognise it as the system the BBC uses to transmit on medium and long waves. The musician using 'tremolo' hears a rapid but slight increase and decrease of loudness of his sound, which perhaps is a more

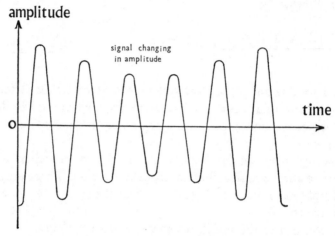

Fig 14   Tremolo

interesting quality. Many early combo amps had a tremolo facility which could be switched in or out of circuit with a footswitch. Most people agree that vibrato is a more interesting effect. Note that the 'tremolo arm' on a guitar actually changes the pitch of the note. Strictly speaking it is a 'vibrato arm'.

TREATING THE FREQUENCY
Vibrato

In the vibrato treatment the frequency of the signal is made to increase and decrease slightly at a frequency of between 5 and 10Hz (see fig 15). Technically this is called 'frequency modulation' or 'FM' and our radio expert will recognise it as the system the BBC uses to transmit VHF radio. Using 'vibrato' you will hear a rapid but slight rise and fall of pitch, which is a lot more interesting than constant pitch.

Most organs include a vibrato circuit to add interest to the sound. One problem here is that the vibrato is either 'on' or 'off' – it comes or goes suddenly. Some organs have two different speeds of vibrato, but, even so, switching from none to one, or from one to the other, still creates a sudden change. Organists

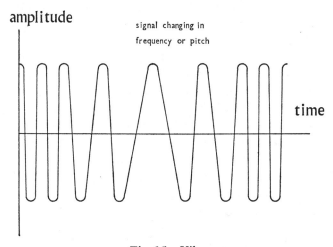

Fig 15   Vibrato

have means of overcoming this (see below). The guitarist, like the violinist or other string player, creates vibrato by a good technique of finger wobble with the left hand; he can also wobble with the right hand on the so-called 'tremolo' arm.

Leslies

This loudspeaker system was conceived by D. J. Leslie in the USA and the name Leslie is now a registered trade mark of CBS Inc in the USA. Leslie's aim apparently was to provide the electric organ with a 'proper' organ sound by creating amplitude, frequency and phase modulation. The sound is made to rotate through 360° by means of a mechanically driven rotor, and the Döppler effect becomes apparent. This is an effect which causes the pitch of a sound to change if the source of sound and the listener are moving relative to one another. In the early Leslie a wooden drum with a loudspeaker mounted on its side rotated about a vertical axis, so that the loudspeaker swept around the circumference of a circle; electrical connections were made through mercury contacts at the top of the vertical shaft, which was belt driven by an electric motor. As the speaker approached the hearer the notes emitted were sharpened; as it receded, they were flattened.

Modern Leslies usually have stationary speaker systems and PTFE rotors of which there may be two – one for bass, and one for the treble horns. All have various speeds – the Leslie 760, for example, can be switched from stationary to slow rotation (or chorale), and on to fast rotation (tremolo) and back again. A good organist attaches great significance to the effect produced to the sound as the rotor accelerates and brakes. Some Leslies have built-in amplifiers; the 760 has 90W of silicon solid state amplification available – but it does weigh 144lb.

We use a Leslie 825, which is slightly less powerful at 70W but only weighs 87lb – a very good compromise for the gig organist. Other instruments, such as guitars, can use Leslies, but they are most commonly associated with organs, in which they are sometimes 'built-in'. There is a whole variety of Leslies, from the small 110 up to the huge 950, which weighs 375lb and incorporates 200W of amplification and four rotors plus a 'spinning graphics light show'.

The Hammond Leslies have their competitors, notably Sondyne tone cabinets from Ling Dynamic Systems Ltd and Electratone from Lowrey. The 'genuine' Leslies also have their electronic imitators, notably the Schaller Rotorsound. With the advance of integrated circuits, major developments may be expected in solid-state Leslie equivalents.

Ring modulators
The ring modulator is a famous telecommunication circuit of many years ago. Today the transformers have been superseded by pure solid state devices, such as the four quadrant multipliers found in the Halo Ringmod (see plate p 119).

Musically, the ring modulator is unique. Two perfectly musical signals can be fed in, and the output can be a totally discordant jangle. So beware.

Basically, a ring modulator is an electronic box that needs two inputs and gives one output. Let us suppose that the input at channel 1 is a perfect sine shape having only the one frequency of 200Hz, and that the input at channel 2 is another perfect sine shape, again having only one frequency, 300Hz. Then the single output contains neither 200Hz nor 300Hz, but consists of two notes, one being 300−200, which is 100Hz, and the other being 300+200, which is 500Hz. So we finish up with a sound consisting of 100Hz and 500Hz, two frequencies neither of which need have any musical connection with either 200Hz or 300Hz.

Let us take this a little further. Replace the 300Hz signal at channel 2 by a complex waveform more like that of a real musical instrument, consisting of the harmonics 300, 600, 900, 1200 and 1500Hz. The 300 ring modulates against the 200 to give 100 and 500 as before. The 600 ring modulates against the 200 to give 400 and 800. The 900 produces 700 and 1100, The 1200 produces 1000 and 1400, and the 1500 produces 1300 and 1700. So our output now is a complex sound containing the harmonics 100, 400, 500, 700, 800, 1000, 1100, 1300, 1400 and 1700Hz, which is some chord. Imagine then the effect if *both* our inputs had been complex waves from musical instruments.

Most synthesisers incorporate a ring modulation facility, often used to produce the characteristic 'electronic music' effects.

But the average musician can use a ring modulator to great

effect. Fig 16 shows how you could play an octave higher in perfect synchronisation with your normal melody line. Here the ring modulator is used to double the frequency of the melody line, adding the octave. Any ring modulator will do this: if the same note of say 300Hz is applied to both inputs the

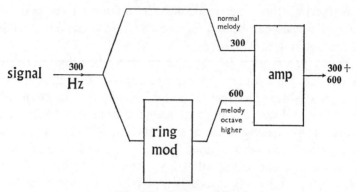

Fig 16   Octave adding

output is 300+300 which is 600Hz (an octave higher) and 300−300 which is zero. The Halo Ringmod is particularly convenient for this because, if channel 1 is used alone, it automatically parallels both inputs. A foot switch is provided to short the Ringmod straight through.

TREATING THE TONE

The tone of a signal can be changed in several ways by altering the harmonic content of the signal. This change can be a dramatic 'on-off' effect, like the treble boost, or it can be a continuous gradual change played by the musician, like the wah-wah effect.

Treble boost

In the treble boost treatment the top or treble end of the harmonics of the tone is amplified considerably, while the

62

middle and bass frequencies are left unchanged. When the footswitch is kicked down the circuit is powered by an internal 9V battery and the top harmonics of the signal are amplified about thirty-five times more than the others, as fig 17 shows. When the footswitch is again kicked down, the signal is shorted

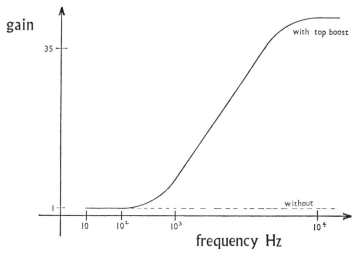

Fig 17   Response curve of treble booster

straight through without any treatment, and the battery switched off. On some instruments you don't have to remember whether you left it on or off because when you pull the jack leads out it switches off automatically. Most commercial circuits comprise a simple single transistor voltage amplifier in which the coupling capacitors are less than one per cent of their normal value, so that the higher frequencies are amplified at the expense of the others.

Wah wah

The wah-wah effect is now very commonly used by most lead guitarists and keyboard men. The device usually takes the physical form of a swell-type foot pedal which, when pressed hard

63

down, activates the circuit from an internal battery; further movement of the pedal up and down brings in either fewer or more harmonics. When the pedal is again pressed hard down the signal goes straight through and the battery is switched off to conserve power. Various filter circuits are involved, each manufacturer having his own. Some use a filter which, as the foot is depressed on the pedal, slowly adds the upper harmonics making the sound slowly more treble on top of the middle and bass already there. This is a variable low-pass filter. Others use a band-pass filter: only a certain band of harmonics is allowed through, and this band can be swept through the audio range from low to high frequency by pressing down the pedal. Halo's version is unique: not only can it be pedal operated, but, as it has an integral light cell, variation in light intensity can be used instead, giving rise to several interesting possibilities of interfacing lights and sounds.

Fuzz

This very popular treatment involves the deliberate distortion of the signal. Usually the device is a fuzz box (see plate p 119) and is operated by the guitarist's foot. The switching is similar to the treble boost box (see above) but may also include a control enabling the musician to vary the amount of distortion, commonly being called the 'depth' of the fuzz.

The principle is shown in fig 18. At (a) we show the small signal from the guitar pick-up, shown for simplicity as a single-frequency or sine wave. At (b) the signal is shown amplified considerably by the first stage of the fuzz box, and (c) shows the effect on the wave in (b) if its amplitude is now limited; the result is a chopped off or distorted signal. By controlling the gain of the amplifying first stage, we can control the angle that the sections marked V make with the time axis, and so control the harmonics added to the signal, or the distortion introduced.

Good fuzz box design is not easy, but there are several good models on the market. Quality of sound is highly subjective –

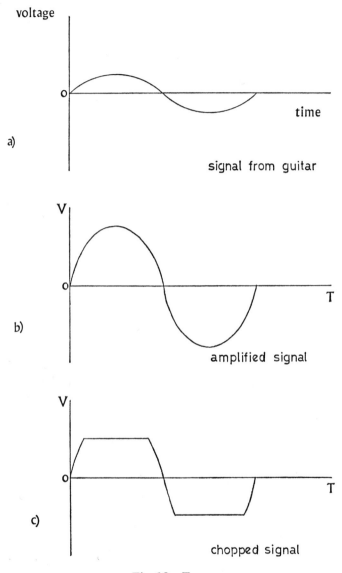

Fig 18   Fuzz

what sounds good to one musician sounds bad to another. There is no alternative really to going in the shop and trying it out yourself, at the volume level you want to use.

Envelope shaping

Just how the sound starts and grows, the length of time it lasts, its decay, and finally the length of time for which it is off, all contribute significantly to the tone of the sound. We simplify this in fig 19 to just four regions – attack, on, decay, and off. There is more about this so-called 'envelope' of a sound in the Appendix (see p 152).

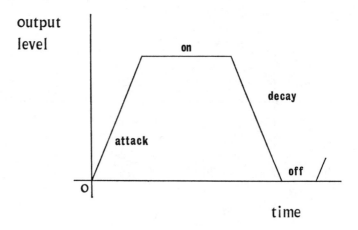

Fig 19   Envelope of a sound

Treatments that artificially change the natural envelope of the sound are fairly new, although most synthesisers have them. In fact, it is the use of the envelope voltage as a control that produces a lot of the special sound effects associated with synthesisers.

TREATING THE SOUND OVERALL

Other treatments can add a feeling of 'space' to the overall sound – as if you are playing in a large empty room. Reverb and echo come in this category, and there is some confusion between these two. Reverberation (or reverb for short) is the repeated reflection of the sound off walls, floors, and so on. It occurs quite soon after the original sound, usually within a second. Echo on the other hand is a very clean repeat of the original and occurs perhaps more than a second later, when the sound travels some distance and then bounces back unconfused by the original sound.

Reverberation and echo
There are four principal ways of generating artificial reverb. The *reverb chamber*, now mainly of historic interest, consists of a special room with very hard walls, none of which are parallel. The signal is fed through a speaker system into the chamber and picked up – with the added reverb of the chamber – by microphone. The quality of reverb is very good and life-like. The drawbacks to the method are the sacrifice of a room solely for this purpose and the difficulty of changing the level of reverb when the room is built (although this can be done).

The *reverb plate* is a steel plate about $2\frac{1}{2} \times 1\frac{1}{2}$m, suspended vertically in its own wooden housing and perforated with small holes to avoid resonances (see Appendix, p 161). The loudspeaker and microphone are placed diagonally opposite each other on the plate. The reverb time is altered by moving a blanket of damping material nearer to the plate to decrease, and further from the plate to increase. This damper can be hand or motor driven and gives a range of reverb times from half a second to five seconds. Again the quality is very good because of the wide range of harmonics which the plate can handle. But reverb plates are expensive and take up a fair bit of space.

The *spring reverb* is the device familiar to most musicians of moderate means. It is commonly fitted to guitar amps, organs and synthesisers. As in both other types a physical medium, usually steel, is used to delay the sound; the steel is arranged as a fine wire and coiled up as a spring to save space. The principle is then the same : the electric signal is converted to a sound wave by a piezo-electric crystal at one end of the spring, and this sound wave travels relatively slowly down the spring where it is transduced back to an electric signal by a similar crystal. There are innumerable reflections of the sound wave backwards and forwards from the ends of the spring, and the overall result is a reasonable reverb sound. The Hammond and Grampian spring units are well known.

As the springs are usually less than half a metre long, the low frequency response is not good. The spring units are also very sensitive to mechanical knocks, and can be set into resonance by high volume levels, but they are compact and the control facilities are convenient.

The *tape loop or drum* is the only pure electronic system. In this system the sound is fed into an endless loop of normal recording tape at a record head. This sound is sent on directly and picked up by successive replay heads so that it is transmitted with various time delays as a reverb or even echo. The tape passes over an erase head before reaching the record head again. Alternatively, the heads can be arranged around the circumference of a rotating magnetic drum. On the better machines the heads are movable. This system gives a compact, economical, versatile and good quality device. The WEM Copycat in the UK and the Binson in the USA are good examples.

Combinations

All of these treatments can be combined. You may want to use a wah-wah pedal and a fuzz box together. Most manufacturers make compatible gear. You may find that you have to reverse the positions of the wah and fuzz treatments between the source and the amp to get best results. An organist using a portable organ and swell pedal wishing to add wah-wah may find it better to put the signal through the wah first and then through the swell pedal or vice versa.

Some manufacturers have combined one or more treatments.

Selmer, for example, have a combined wah and fuzz pedal. The Jennings 'Scrambler' combines top boost, bass boost, fuzz, wah, and swell or volume in one foot control unit. The Maestro W-3 is a very advanced woodwind sound system enabling a suitably bugged saxophone player to simulate the sounds of oboe, cor anglais etc, and one or two octaves below normal if he wishes. All synthesisers contain a large number of treatments, as we shall see in Chapter 7.

Chapter 4

THE STAGE SET-UP

We have examined in some detail the currently available electric and electronic instruments and their construction. Now we shall look at their use in combination within a typical stage set-up as utilised by many professional musicians. The exact configuration and layout will be largely determined by considerations of the equipment available, number of performers, etc; but we can lay down some general guide lines applicable to almost any situation involving electric instruments.

In fig 20 we have shown a typical small band arrangement, using drums, bass guitar, lead guitar and organ. Vocals are handled by the lead and bass guitarists. This simple set-up includes a drum kit, at this stage still acoustic, guitar amp and speaker cabinet, bass amp and cabinet, organist's amp/speaker combination, and a simple 'public address system' or PA involving two mikes, amp and two speaker columns (perhaps with additional horn tweeters). There is no real sophistication involved, control of each instrument being entirely independent; but even at this simple level (which is common to many if not most small bands throughout the country) a lot can be done to ensure the best sound.

The general positioning is worthy of careful study. The players are situated mid-stage, where they can see each other. The guitarists have a clear path both to the front and rear of

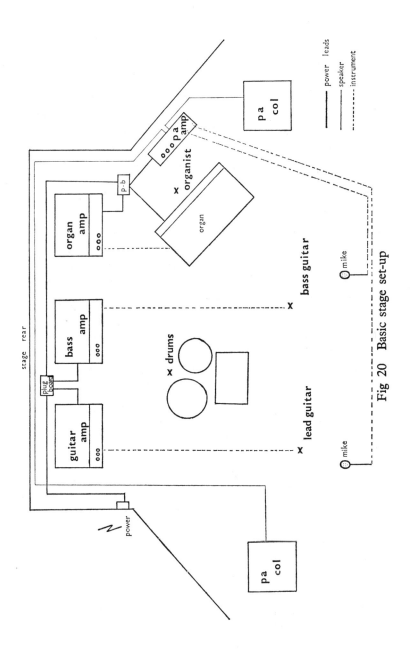

Fig 20 Basic stage set-up

power leads
speaker
instrument

pa col

pa amp

organist

x

organ amp

organ

p-b

bass guitar

bass amp

x

drums

x

lead guitar

x

guitar amp

mike

mike

plug board

stage rear

power

pa col

their section of stage, so that they can easily reach their micro-phones and their amplifiers are readily accessible to them for adjustment. When in position stage front and using the mikes, the PA columns are slightly behind them, so that they can hear their own vocals. The PA will often be almost completely inaudible to the band if the musicians are behind its speakers; the drummer and organist may therefore be at a severe disadvantage. It is obviously of prime importance that the players must be able to hear all the musical lines.

The drummer, it will be noticed, is positioned well forward, and is thus in a good position to hear the instrument amplification behind him. The organist has the PA amp close at hand and can readily make adjustments if required. And what of the sound the audience hears? The simple answer is that the band, while they are on stage, has no sure way of telling whether it is good, bad or indifferent. With no mixing or monitoring system they must either rely on audience comment between sets or ensure they have a helpful friend in the hall who can make signals as appropriate. The best solution to the problem, even with a small-scale set-up, is to arrive at the venue in good time to balance the sound thoroughly before the audience arrives; little adjustment should then be required during performance.

We will now turn to more specific aspects of setting up the gear, and go on to outline some rather more advanced techniques.

AMPS AND STACKS

Once the gear is unloaded from the band's transport and dragged unwillingly to the stage, setting up can begin; it is wise not to rush headlong into this, but to size up the situation as an essential preliminary. Very often, for reasons of size of stage, strange room acoustics, or lack of co-operation on the part of the management, it will not be possible to attain our ideal stage set-up.

One of the first difficulties to arise is usually obtaining a power supply; the best method is to have a long wandering lead (at least 30ft) terminating in a plug board with about six outlets. It is the other end of this lead which will often produce a ripe selection of the musician's favourite curses, for that is the end that must mate with whatever socket the particular venue possesses. You will find the most bizarre and heathen things still lurking in forgotten corners of village halls, daring you to extract a meagre watt from their cobwebbed exterior: 15amp, 5amp, even 2amp, everything except the 'standard' 13amp flat pin fused with which you will be sensibly equipped. The solution is to carry one of each of these plugs, and change when necessary. There are various multi-way plugs available, but we must confess we have found none of them very satisfactory in prolonged use; in any case, since a single point only is involved, the additional labour is fairly minimal. Two don'ts: *never* stick leads into a socket with matchsticks in the absence of a plug; and *refuse* absolutely to perform if only two-pin or light sockets are available. If you want to stay alive, use a three-pin point and make certain that it is earthed.

Having got our power to the stage area, we can connect up the amplifiers and instruments. Most amps will have a mains lead of about six to ten feet; this should terminate in a flat-pin plug fused at 2amp, which is connected on to the plug board. If our amps are a fair distance apart on a larger stage, we may need to split the plug board into two or more sections. Keep the wires and all other leads neat and tidy, out of the way of feet; if you have time, tape all the leads neatly on to the stage, grouped together in their various runs. The dangers here are obvious: tripping over a lead can physically injure the tripper or damage his instrument, or, more lethally, pull out an earth wire from a plug. If the wire involved is an instrument or speaker lead, the show may literally stop as silence descends (except for the drummer who will inevitably still be playing). Leads of this type may be loosely tied round a convenient handle before entering the amp or speaker; then, though the victim may be

73

crushed by the heavy cabinet he has pulled down on to him, at least the show goes on.

Amps with separate speakers must next be connected to them; use fairly heavy two-core cable with appropriate connectors, not co-ax instrument leads. Always connect speaker leads before switching on the amp; otherwise something may melt. Speakers will usually be matched correctly to amp output impedances, if both units are from the same manufacturer; some amplifiers have various output tappings on the back, but very few speaker cabinets have their impedances marked on them. Most common are 16ohm, 8ohm and sometimes 4ohm; mis-matching can lose a lot of power and cause damage and distortion, particularly to transistor amps. If in doubt, and if the amp impedance is known, whip the back off the cabinet and look at the speakers. Usually the impedance of individual speakers will be marked on them, along with their power rating; according to their wiring, whether it be in series or parallel (see fig 21), we can work out the total impedance of the cabinet. Two rules: if wired in series, add the impedances to arrive at the total; if in parallel, and all speakers are rated at the same impedance, divide by

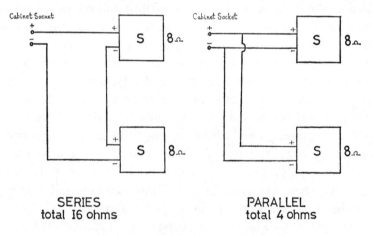

SERIES
total 16 ohms

PARALLEL
total 4 ohms

Fig 21   Speaker cabinet impedance

the number of speakers. Thus two 8ohm speakers in series gives us a loading of sixteen ohms; in parallel, one of four ohms.

Having laid all our power lines and connected the speakers, we can switch on the amps and let them warm up; in the case of transistor amps this warm-up period is unnecessary. Most valve amps these days have a separate mains switch to keep the valves warm, and a stand-by switch to activate the high-tension circuit when we want to start playing. Always allow a minute or so of warm-up before switching in the stand-by. Most systems, unless they are very luxurious, will emit a gentle hum while they are working; but excessive background noise should be investigated, and will often indicate a fault condition. Some bands are forced to play at a nerve shattering volume merely to drown the hiss and hum emanating from their amps.

A common cause of mains hum is the duplication of earth leads on organs and other instruments with their own power supply, causing earth loops. Disconnect all except one earth lead within the affected instrument's set-up, ensuring that there is a continuous earth path via the outer braid of the signal co-ax (fig 22). If in doubt about the correct way to do this, ask a competent audio engineer; mistakes could be fatal if you leave

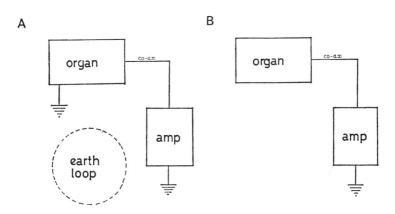

Fig 22   Earth loops

yourself unearthed. It has been known for guitarists to be electrocuted via the strings and the casing of a mike which has gone live due to an earth fault on the PA. This won't happen to you if you keep your gear in good nick, check all leads regularly, and ensure that your power supply on the stand is above reproach. As an additional safety measure, guitarists can buy a small fused connector which hooks into their instrument line, and affords protection against this sort of fault.

Instrument leads are the next to consider (they go in the little holes in the amp). Their varieties will be manifold, according to the instrument served; most usual is coiled pvc-covered co-ax, with ¼in jacks on each end. Metal jacks are better than the all-moulded variety; at least they can be repaired when the lead breaks down. And they are more robust for those with big feet. If you have lots of fuzz boxes and pedals, you can make up short lengths to connect them with straight co-ax and screened jacks; keep all connections nice and tight, preferably soldered, and you will have no trouble with hum or nasty silences at the wrong moment.

Many amplifiers have the facility for adding a slave amp (with extra speakers) to increase the power output; if you are using these, simply follow the maker's instructions. There is a simple way of slaving if you have available spare amplifiers not specifically designed for the job. From a spare input on the channel you are using on your own amp, run a co-ax lead to the input on the spare (see fig 23). This is not true slaving, merely running the two amps in parallel, but it will boost your sound by the output of the second amp; a similar result can be obtained by running a 'Y' lead from the instrument.

There has been a noticeable trend in recent years for bands to play at much greater overall volumes, necessitating ever more powerful amplifiers, more speaker cabinets, amplified drums, etc. A look at some early Beatle shots will quickly confirm this; two AC 30s and that's about your lot! This presents many problems, not the least of which is financial; and of course, this year's number one gear is next year's outdated, not loud enough 'trade-in'. All of which keeps our music industry very happy. But do you really need more power? If you are being drowned by other instruments, then a better quality amp with greater

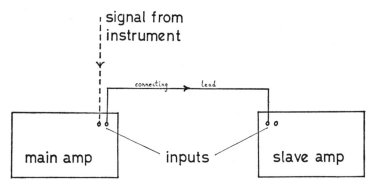

Fig 23   Slaving with spare amps

clarity, not necessarily more power, could be a more logical answer. And if, in fact, your overall volume is not sufficient for the larger venues, then a far more sensible scheme is to buy a large scale PA with comprehensive facilities for the whole band, and mike your small amp through that. The PA can always be uprated and added to later, if it is any good at all. Often large single amps are very disappointing in terms of sound from a guitarist's point of view, as he likes to drive his amp hard to get sustain, a practice which is far more controllable with amps of around 30–50W.

Note that when we talk in terms of electrical power output, ie watts, be they peak, RMS or whatever, 100W is not twice as loud as 50W – only about ten per cent louder. And remember, no amplifier will compensate for deficient tone production at the instrumentalist's fingers.

One last point; at the end of the gig, let your valve amps cool thoroughly before throwing them into the van. The glass valves will be duly grateful.

77

MIKES AND PA

The term public address system or PA is in this context a hangover from the days when performers depended on a fixed installation in the venue, which in turn was (and often still is) little better than a railway station announcer's rig. Such crude devices are best ignored altogether. Here we shall discuss portable (well, almost) PA systems, which are really voice amplification set-ups as distinct from instrument types. The main difference is that PA involves a mechanical transducer, ie the microphone, rather than a magnetic transducer (as with guitars) or none at all (organs, synthesisers).

The simplest possible PA is a mike and a small amp, such as a Vox AC 30. Plug it in and away you go; but very soon you will run into problems. Whereas the same amp with a guitar running through it produces a satisfactory volume level, with a mike it seems impossible to get above the band; and any attempts to increase volume are thwarted by that howling menace, *feedback*. One point that becomes immediately evident, then, is that generally speaking we will need about twice as much power on our PA as the total of the instrument amplifiers, to enable a correct balance to be obtained.

Here some remarks on feedback and associated problems seem called for; the following comments are applicable in essence to *any* system.

Feedback is really a self-perpetuating signal, a condition which arises when an initial signal (in this case, a movement of the microphone diaphragm), instead of decaying, is continued or increased by air movement from the amplifier loudspeakers; the result is a howl or whistle, which will continue until the cycle is broken by switching the power off, or reducing the amplifier gain (see fig 24). Reduction or elimination of feedback consists in essence of an alteration in the set-up, significant enough to break the cycle. Something as simple as standing between the microphone and the speakers can often be effective.

78

For the moment we will discount the effects of room acoustics and consider the equipment in isolation. Of course, it is a simple matter to stop feedback; we just turn the amplifier volume down. But usually this will be inconvenient or downright impossible, because the PA will no longer be audible and the balance of the band be disrupted; the problem is to remove the feedback condition while maintaining or even increasing the PA volume.

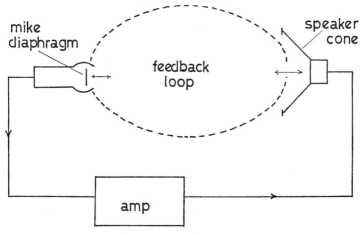

Fig 24   Feedback cycle

Positioning of the mikes in relation to the speakers is the first point to consider. They must certainly not be placed directly in front (try pointing a live mike at the speakers close in for a convincing demonstration). This does create practical problems, however, due to small stages and the necessity, already discussed, for the performers to hear themselves. A compromise is usually best, therefore, with the mikes slightly in front and to one side of the speakers (see fig 20). Suitable microphones for band PA help us here; in general they should be of the cardioid type (moving coil or condenser), which will have a tight acceptance angle and high unwanted signal rejection (see fig 25). Suitable models are produced by Shure, AKG, Beyer, etc. When we come later to more sophisticated systems, our microphone options will naturally have to be a little more diverse.

The other main area over which we have control is the amplifier, and more particularly the filter settings thereon. Feedback comes in two different packs; type one is a high pitched whistle, type two a low pitched howl; it is generally

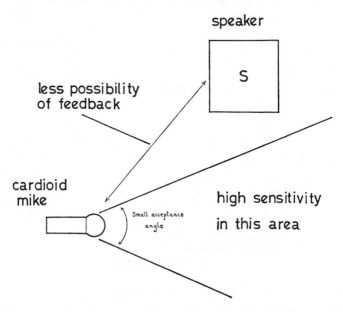

Fig 25 Use of cardioid microphones

possible to cure the first by reducing the treble boost at the amp, and the second by removing some of the bass boost. This, if carried to its logical conclusion, will of course result in a thin tinny sound, like the Vicar opening the village fête, so some discretion is advised. Another useful maxim for avoiding feedback; if you have too bassy a sound, don't increase the treble boost, but roll off some of the bass instead – and vice versa, of course.

Room acoustics involve us in further complications, none of which we can do much about. If the venue itself has a nasty resonance (see Appendix, p 161), and you excite it rather than the audience, then no amount of fiddling is going to save you. Play softer, and think about the next gig. And then there are all the possible interactions between the mikes and the instrument speakers, which are quite evilly disposed to set up a nasty low resonance, occurring only while you are bashing away, and therefore difficult to diagnose. Helpful tip: switch off all mikes when not in use during performance. To sum up; feedback, while an inherent bogey in any unmonitored, unmixed system, can be reduced by intelligent application of the foregoing principles, provided that once it's right, you leave it alone.

So far, we have been talking only in terms of the most basic of systems, a power amp with around four inputs and one set of tone filters, feeding out to a pair of columns containing a set of four identical heavy-duty speakers each; pretty unsophisticated, but still common enough. Better amps exist, however, to drive our columns, having full mixing facilities over four or more channels, with separate tone filters for each; more speaker outlets will usually be available, together with a slave output (enabling power to be increased later when required). These features obviously benefit us tremendously when balancing the PA, and enable an individual treatment of each mike input to be readily achieved. Better loudspeaker enclosures will help matters, too, and indeed are essential if we intend to mike instruments through the set-up; providing a wider frequency response and greater clarity necessitates the use of multi-speaker systems with a proper crossover network, incorporating low, mid, and high range units (see plate p 34). Today, working bands make use of considerably further advanced equipment, but this properly belongs in the next section, along with stereo techniques.

To conclude, a word regarding echo and reverberation devices. These were described on pp 67-8, and allow us to obtain various combinations of, in effect, 'distance' from untreated sounds. Straight delayed echo can be used to devastating effect on vocals (hear Robert Plant), and a tasteful application of reverberation can broaden and give depth to choruses, solo instruments etc. The possibilities are limited only by taste and imagination, and of course are displayed to their best advantage when applied in a 'dead' acoustic environment; this enables a proper layering effect to be obtained, where the various instruments are separated by degrees of apparent distance.

All these devices have one disadvantage in common, however; for a given level of output volume, their use increases the probability of feedback. This tendency increases with the amount of 'depth' applied at the unit. Poorly made and designed units will also do little to enhance the music, with their extraneous hiss and noise; and in a venue which has a tendency to boom or echo, the use of reverb is just plain silly, as of course is its indiscriminate use in any situation. The usual reason for the over-use of echo is lack of talent on the part of the band; if your vocals are thin and out of pitch, the proper course of action is (i) learn to sing, (ii) get a vocalist, (iii) (if all else fails) give it a bit more echo! Judging from the sound that some bands produce, all else has obviously failed.

MIXING AND MONITORING

This section must start with fig 26, showing our advanced stage set-up, and to obtain a proper understanding of the techniques involved we will refer to it throughout. On stage, we have for the sake of clarity kept the number of players to a minimum; the system is of course readily flexible and can accommodate any number of players, given sufficient input channels at the mixer. Our band will now have to include another essential member, the sound engineer, whose function will be to balance, monitor, and present to the audience the musical intentions of the on-stage performers.

The guitarists use only small amplifiers, in themselves

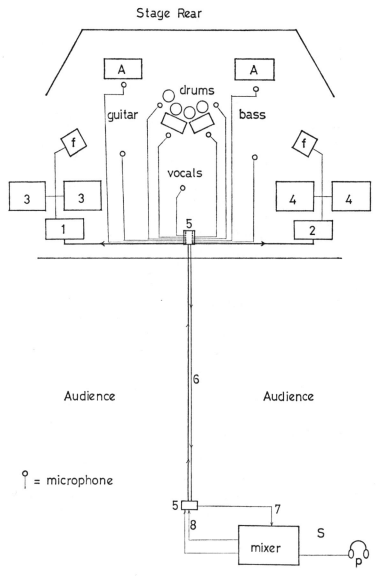

Fig 26 Advanced stage set-up

KEY
1: left-hand power amp   5: junction box
2: right-hand power amp   6: multi-way cable
3: LH PA bins and horns   7: unmixed inputs
4: RH PA bins and horns   8: balanced outputs
A: instrument amplifier   p: headphones for monitoring
f: foldback enclosure   S: sound engineer

completely insufficient to fill the (presumably) large hall, but having the required sustain, tonal characteristics, etc. These amps are miked up with cardioid equipment, the mikes in line with the speaker axis mounted on reversed boom stands. Vocal mikes of similar pattern are stage front, three in number; these can also serve for doubles such as flutes, saxes etc if required. If the band should include brass or woodwind players on a regular basis, these will of course be accommodated by specific extra mikes; if such players use bugs for pickup, the lines from these can run back to the mixer with the rest. The drums and any additional percussion are miked up according to the requirements of the particular musicians; in general, an omnidirectional mike should be suspended above the cymbals, with separate cardioid mikes near the individual tom-toms, snare, bass drums and so forth. At this level of expertise (and expense!) it is well worth matching microphones to specific tasks, eg a suitable mike for the bass guitar will have a response curve tailored to the frequency range of that instrument. Studio mikes, if handled with the necessary care, can produce cleaner results on vocals and horns than the usual, more rugged, group items; all the leading manufacturers will be pleased to advise on suitable models for specific applications.

On our diagram we have shown the mixer at the rear of the hall; this is the most logical position for our sound engineer in many ways, since he can easily assess the overall volume and balance of the band. This is not absolutely essential, of course, and imposes some restrictions on the set-up; the engineer must have advance notice of the band's intentions, since he cannot easily communicate with them, and the microphones used must be of the low-impedance type, since the lines to the mixer will be very long. These lines run from the stage to a junction box, and then to the rear of the hall via a single multi-way cable, which also carries the final signal back to the power amplifiers. Another junction box separates the mike lines, which are then fed to the mixer inputs.

Mixers, as previously described in Chapter 2, basically accept a number of input signals and allow them to be individually balanced and filtered, presenting a single output to the power amplifier. A little greater sophistication is required in this application, however, and the mixers used are closer to a portable version of a studio desk than a normal PA set-up. There will normally be between five to ten input channels, each with two input sockets, separate gain and filter controls applying to each channel. Other facilities will include reverberation, VU meters for monitoring output levels, headphone sockets, and a master volume control; output will be into two channels for stereo operation (see plate p 34). The sound engineer can balance the incoming signals via the headphones and meters without feeding any sound to the speaker enclosures, thus simplifying pre-performance setting up.

It may seem unnecessary to use any on-stage amplifiers at all, since with the system described it is technically possible simply to run the guitar signal back to the mixer along with the rest, and remove the additional complexity of re-miking on-stage amps. This is not advised, however, as the electric guitar and amplifier should be regarded as a unit, instrumentalists using techniques of overload and distortion for specific musical effects, which they cannot do when control of the amplifier is removed from the player; the engineer is responsible for the level of these instruments, therefore, but not for their tonal characteristics, which remain in the hands of the player. In the studio things may be otherwise, as we shall see.

Our balanced and monitored signal, in two channels (left and right for stereo), now runs back to the stage area via the multi-way cable and junction boxes. There it is fed to the two power amplifiers, which can be of any rated output, as desired; around 500–1500W is common. These amps may be valve or solid state, but should have good linearity and low distortion factors; no filters are required. High power solid state amps will require adequate cooling, small fans sometimes being a desirable accessory. From these amps the right- and left-hand speaker enclosures are fed.

Speaker enclosures in use at present are a far cry from our simple PA columns. Bass frequencies are fed to folded horn bass-bins, front-loaded with one high power (150W) 15in speaker. Mid and high frequencies go out through sectorial horns, electronic crossover units separating the frequencies and completing the set-up (see plate p 51). These enclosures will be arranged either side of the stage, in multiples sufficient to handle the power output of the amplifiers; speakers of this type are very efficient in terms of sound pressure generated for volts input, and effectively restrict the radiation of the output to the frontal plane. To enable the band to hear themselves, small foldback enclosures are placed on-stage and fed at a low level from the main amps. If the number of output channels from the mixer is increased to four, more speakers can be placed at the sides or rear of the hall to give a multi-channel 'surround sound' effect; panning facilities at the mixer, where the signal can be swept smoothly from one channel to the next, will add to the possible use which can be made of such an expanded system.

To sum up the advantages of this more sophisticated system of band amplification: correct balance and an appropriate level of volume is assured (given a competent sound engineer), and feedback is eliminated. Variables of hall acoustics are more readily dealt with, and a proper spatial separation of the instruments is made possible by a correct stereophonic sound image. In essence, the set-up is identical to that in a recording studio, the signal being fed from the mixing desk to amps and speakers rather than on to tape. The principal disadvantage is obviously one of cost; it is in some measure offset by the ease with which such a system may be expanded or up-rated at any time, without the costly necessity of scrapping the original components, which are simply added to and remain as the nucleus of the set-up.

Transport of these large PAs is another difficulty, requiring a large truck and permanently employed roadies, whose sole job is to shift and set up the gear; setting up itself is a lengthy operation, requiring possession of the venue for the day prior to the performance. The results, however, can more than justify the extra effort involved.

TRANSPORT AND MAINTENANCE

First transport for most of us consists of borrowing or begging a lift in father's/elder brother's/friend's car. Involvement with a working band on a fairly regular basis, means that some form of group transport to cover the needs of all the players becomes an essential, and the band van arrives. Even the most obscure, unknown, only-play-on-Saturdays local group is likely to have its own van, proudly emblazoned with the name of our heroes written large on each side, and strange indeed are many of those names; 'The Cruds', perhaps, or 'Concrete Icicle', or worse. Inside the truth is stranger still; could we but open those twisted rusting doors, a mountain of huge black cabinets rises to the roof; every other inch of available space is packed tight with mike stands, guitars, cable, boxes containing drums and cymbals – and just visible, barely discernible in the all pervading gloom, squashed into the last centimetres of available space, are the members of our band. And these same wretches will at the end of their nightmare ride be expected to leap out, carry mountains of gear up steps, wire up, balance the sound, and spring into vibrant action before an indifferent crowd who only turned up because the disco was closed. So one of the basic priorities is to ensure that the chosen transport has sufficient capacity for the gear *and* the players, in reasonable comfort. A van with side windows and proper seats is vital if long journeys are to be undertaken; such vehicles will have between 15 to 30cwt capacity, be reasonably cheap to run, and relatively easy to park and manoeuvre.

When the amount of equipment utilised by the band begins

to exceed that which they can manhandle and still be fresh enough to play, a road manager becomes essential; his job will be to drive the van, lug the gear, help set up, and smooth out any frictions with the venue management. This leaves the players free to concentrate on performing, and benefits the band enormously. The roadie should be a paid member of the band, as even the biggest mug is not going to go hefting gear for free on a regular basis.

Assuming that our van has arrived at the gig, and nothing vital has been forgotten, the two operations at each end of actually playing deserve consideration.

Getting in: parking can be difficult, but remember that you can leave the van on double yellow lines providing that you are actually loading or unloading. Before commencing this operation, send out a scout to check with the management (a) where the band is to play and (b) which is the shortest route to the stage. Neglecting either of these points can result in setting up twice over, or hauling large pieces of equipment twice as far as necessary. Never leave an open van or any gear unattended; that is an open invitation to theft.

Getting out: it is always a good idea to let the audience get out of the way first. Make sure you have got the money. If you have no roadie, and one of the band must drive the van home, it is lunatic to do so when exhausted, half-drunk and dispirited; give yourselves a chance, find a café, relax for a while with coffee and at least be in reasonable condition to tackle the most lethal part of the whole business. Similarly, make it a habit to check lights, brakes, tyres, etc before every trip. If you have a roadie/driver, then it is of course obligatory that he should be a model of sober integrity, and not swelling the bar profits all evening.

Larger bands and fully professional groups with big PAs will need bigger transport, three-ton trucks (usually hired) being commonly used; and of course the number of non-performing employees will also increase, as will the areas of specialisation within the set-up. Roadies will be needed to move the gear, electronics experts to attend to the amplification, a lighting engineer, costume and wardrobe managers, etc. The band at this stage of the game no longer travels with the gear, of course, but in their chauffered Rolls or private plane (one each, preferably). Remember that you can always hire a van, and that if you work only occasionally this can be a lot cheaper than owning a vehicle; PA and amplification can also be hired in the larger cities, and so can whole road crews for tours and so forth. Always remember to insure your equipment, and insure your van to carry it; the small premium required can save a large outlay in replacing stolen gear at a later date.

Maintenance of the gear is undertaken all too often only when a breakdown has already happened. It should be a regular routine for every working band to check its gear over, a knowledgeable person being required of course. Never assume that anyone is qualified for the job unless he has proved his worth. Obvious areas for self-help are as follows: mains leads should be examined for damage and for neat and correct entry to plugs and sockets; fuses should be at two amps, and spares always carried. All other leads and lines should receive regular attention. Amplifiers and mixers should not be tampered with unless you know about their workings; they are very reliable these days, and should be looked at occasionally by a qualified engineer. Speaker cabinets should be stored in dry conditions. Use the covers provided for the equipment always; microphones and other delicate gear should be packed and handled with care. Common sense and sympathetic treatment will make breakdowns a rarity on stage; for those occasions when the gods are not smiling on you, we have a special section on breakdowns in Chapter 5.

Chapter 5
PERFORMANCE

To recapitulate briefly: we have the instruments themselves (the sources), we have the amplifiers and loudspeakers to make them audible, and we have set up our equipment on a stage ready to perform. From this point on we might assume that the players will know their job and can safely be left to get on with it, while we busy ourselves in the rest of the book with the wonders of advanced circuitry and suchlike. The sad fact is, however, that many musicians, once they have been let loose on stage with all this gear, forget about the original purpose of the exercise; so we will take this opportunity of reminding the reader that he should PLAY MUSIC, and discuss a few of the problems involved in performing on various electric instruments. One point which we must clear up immediately: if you play or have played an acoustic instrument in the past, and now must change to an amplified version of that instrument (ie piano to electric piano, saxophone to sax with bug) you must not expect the electric instrument to respond in the same way or to be playable on the same terms. There is a whole new technique to be learned, with some disadvantages and many new possibilities, and to pretend otherwise can only lead to disappointment and frustration. If you play an electric anything, we would urge you to PLAY ELECTRIC, THINK ELECTRIC. Utilise the medium, don't fight it.

The electric guitar

No one can explain the intricacies of playing any instrument in a book. The only way to experience the mental and physical demands involved in performance is actually to perform; one hour's stage experience is worth more than all the books that have ever been written on instrumental technique. Note that we say *stage* experience; practice and rehearsal are obviously necessary and useful, but do not teach you anything about people and performing to them. The audience imposes on the player a host of demands and responsibilities, most of them not directly considered but relevant none the less. The expert player will realise this, perhaps at a subconscious level, and will ensure that he has the technique side of the job under control to the extent that he no longer has to worry about it; he is then free to concentrate his abilities on the part of the job that matters, communication.

The electric guitar has so many possibilities, moods, textures, tones; it is in many ways the most directly expressive electric instrument, and the most versatile. It can play almost any conceivable role within a band: percussively rhythmic, sustaining lines, or washing broad harmonic textures through the music. Arriving at any given mood requires much experience, but the attainment of a given sound *can* be nailed down to practical functions to some extent. Certain things we must take for granted. The most obvious is the instrument itself; a cheap guitar will be a limited tool, capable of little tonal variation and often physically tiring to play. The development of real instrumental technique requires a guitar to match your aspirations.

Strings have the largest direct bearing on the tone of the guitar, after the pickups themselves, and their choice is often a sadly neglected area. If you play in a dance band, or play mostly chords and rhythm, heavy or medium gauge strings will produce a full tone and stay well in pitch; tape or flat-wound strings will give a very plummy smooth sound, with few

91

harmonics, whereas the more usual round-wound strings are brighter in tone and generally more lively. Lead players in rock and blues bands will use a much lighter gauge string, usually with a plain third, and the actual strings can be bought singly in various diameters, the set being made up to personal preference. A typical set would have the following diameters, from the first downwards: 0·009in, 0·011in, 0·014in, 0·022in, 0·030in, and 0·038in. For comparison, the sixth string of a medium-heavy gauge set might have a diameter of 0·058in. A medium gauge set can be used by discarding the sixth, moving each string down one slot, and adding a 0·009in first. Very light gauge strings of this type are essential for modern lead techniques, and put tone production right at the fingertips of the player, who must work a lot harder to produce a tone than with heavy strings; in compensation, his control of expression is greatly enhanced.

Sustain can be obtained in several ways. A good electric guitar will sustain naturally anyway, but finger technique can increase the duration considerably; firm pressure, a certain amount of vibrato, and a 'feel' for the string must be developed. Feedback produces sustain, but usually only on certain pitches and their octaves, and is thus of limited use. Overload distortion, obtained by running the amplifier flat out, produces good results but tends to be restricted in use to very loud playing. It can also be very tricky to control, if the sound is not to blur into a mass of feedback; the strings not being played must be damped with the heel of the hand. Fuzz boxes will produce amazing sustain at any level of volume, but reduce clarity. Using a wah pedal in combination with the fuzz at a constant setting will chop some of the harmonics off the signal, cleaning up the sound in the process; and the wah pedal, if its output is high enough, can increase sustain used on its own. Remember that the wah pedal can be used as a tone filter, and can be left in one position to produce a desired effect. All these techniques will increase the tendency to feedback and muddying if the strings other than the one being picked are allowed to vibrate, and so right-hand technique must be developed to cope.

Control is the ultimate objective of all practice; and physical control of the facilities on the instrument is of vital importance. Get to know your volume and tone filters, and their effect; if you have a pickup selector, practice switching till you no longer have to look for it, and can hit it in between beats. Practice sustain by moving the guitar close into the speakers to induce feedback; be able to select foot pedals and switches for effects without breaking the smooth flow of the passage you are playing. In general, *don't fiddle*: once you have set up the filters and controls on the amplifier, you should not have to alter them. Be able to control your variations of dynamics and texture from the guitar while playing, either from the fingers or via effects pedals. All this may sound a little dogmatic, but it is not intended so; if your music and your sound involve acting differently, by all means do so. Breaking the rules should always be to a musical purpose, and not the result of laziness or lack of effort.

The bass guitar

Producing fundamentals down to 35Hz, the bass guitar places heavy demands on the amplifier/speaker enclosure used, and the achievement of a good sound at realistic volume levels involves the use of first-class equipment. There is little satisfaction to be had from playing bass when the bottom string is virtually unusable, as is all too often the case with inferior equipment; the bass is the bottom of the band, and should produce clean tones down to bottom E without cabinet resonance or undue distortion. One of the snags attached to playing bass is therefore a physical one, that your gear is going to be big and heavy. Cabinets do not necessarily have to contain large drive units, but the enclosure should certainly be massive in construction and large in volume, thus avoiding resonances and allowing a low fundamental vibration rate. And the instrument itself is usually a heavy brute, its weight tending to induce a lop-sided physical development in the player; the muscles in the left hand must be strong for stamina, more so than is needed for guitar. Strangely enough, despite the foregoing, bass players do not in general conform to an expected type, seven feet tall and with a muscular development to send Charles Atlas back to his chest-expander.

Strings for the bass vary as for the guitar, heavy to light gauge, flat or round wound. With one major difference: they are a lot more expensive. A word here on string replacement may not come amiss: despite the manufacturer's dire warnings, wound strings can last a long long time, given a little care and attention after each use. Always wipe the strings clean (underneath as well) before putting the guitar away: wiping the strings with a rag soaked in light machine oil before playing will help their preservation and reduce squeaks from the fingers on round-wound strings. Plain strings on guitars don't seem to last very long, however, losing their pitch; but then they are cheap enough.

Bass guitar can be played with the first two fingers of the right hand, like pizzicato double bass, or with a plectrum, like guitar; the plectrum will produce a more percussive, less legato sound. Try both. Wah pedal can be nice with bass, and can be useful as a foot-controlled tone filter, but fuzz boxes do not seem to suit it. In general, there is no point in trying to outblow the lead guitarist: the bass should usually play its own role, in which simplicity is the major component.

The electric organ
It is difficult to discuss organ-playing in detail, as the many manufacturers' products are so diverse as to be regarded almost as different instruments. The organ itself is a bulky item of equipment, and amplification capable of doing justice to its range will be equally big and heavy; in these days the organist has tended to become a keyboard player, handling electric piano

and possibly synthesiser also. Versatility of technique and approach should therefore distinguish this paragon, not least of his virtues being the realisation that the percussive approach essential for piano does not apply to the organ, which demands a separate ethos entirely.

With so much sound at his command, via usually two manuals and a bass pedal board, it is fatally easy for the unthinking, or plain aggressive, player to swamp out the rest of the band entirely with a great sickly mire of sound, filling up every available space with his turgid notes to the point where the other musicians might as well go home. Economy of sound should be the key and watchword for every player; simply because he possesses every effect from 16ft bass to fire siren and heavenly choir is not reason enough to use them all at once, through every number. But of course you are not that sort of organist, as you display by your outstanding perception and good taste in reading this book.

If the Hammond is the ultimate choice in organs, then it is equally true that most players will aspire to a Leslie cabinet for amplification: usually containing a built in amplifier, the Leslie will enhance the tone of almost any organ. They have only one disadvantage, besides their bulk: in loud bands they tend to lack projection in the frontal plane compared with, say, the guitarist's stack, and thus lose apparent volume on solo lines. This problem is most easily overcome by miking up the Leslie and running out through a large PA system, using the Leslie on stage as a monitor for the band.

The synthesiser
The synthesiser has as yet no recognised or established techniques for its use on stage; in the studio it is of course allied to proved and generally used multitrack recording methods. There are two ways of using the instrument with a band, apart from having resource to prerecorded tapes made up at leisure: the synthesiser may be linked to a keyboard and played in a more or less

conventional fashion, rather like an organ, or the patchboard and oscillator etc controls may be played directly to produce various textures and sounds not directly comparable with conventional musical sounds. It should be remembered that the keyboard itself does not necessarily have to produce a conventional scale, or even notes as such; it can be linked to actuate any of the sounds produced by the device. One snag with the live use of the instrument is the inability on some machines to play more than one note at once, or a combination of sounds simultaneously. This reduces its value somewhat, as compared with its use in a studio situation, where it can be allied to tape in a very creative fashion. This of course is no reason for precluding its use on stage; but as far as technique goes, you are very much on your own, with every possibility open and fresh to conquer. This in itself makes its use an attractive proposition.

Balance

Achieving a good internal balance within a band requires practice like any other facet of playing, the basic requirement being one of a continuous awareness of and sensitivity to the changing dynamic demands of the music. It must be admitted that balance in an electric band is by no means easy, the usual problem being the inability to hear the other instruments properly due to the necessary directional properties of the speaker systems in use. A good monitor system, if only for the vocals and brass, is of inestimable value.

One of the easiest traps for a band to fall into is the *volume spiral* (ever upwards). One player rises above the band on a solo for example; the rest of the band follow suit, another musician is drowned out and he reacts by raising *his* volume above the band's new level. The process is repeated until everyone is playing flat out all the time; the drummer, who without mikes has no retaliatory power, is by this time half dead with exhaustion and inaudible anyway. The cure is to realise that, just because one player has risen in dynamic level, that does not imply that you all must: who knows, he may be trying to introduce a little dynamic range into the performance. A complete answer is provided by a full-scale PA with a proper mixing desk, but then balance is put squarely on the shoulders of the sound engineer, who may or may not be worthy of his task.

Effects and treatments
Boxes, boxes, boxes; the stage around our hero's feet is littered with them, a vast untidy mess of creaking pedals, crackling footswitches, and frayed leads ready to trip the unwary into our adoring audience, who would doubtless appreciate this opportunity to examine their idol more closely. Two essentials, then; all effects boxes should be the best you can afford, their switch-gear and pots silent in operation, and they should not impede the flow of your performance but enhance it. The use to which the various treatments are put, wah, fuzz, echo or whatever, is largely a matter of taste. Listen to the masters of technique like Hendrix and Zappa for ideas on how to use a wah pedal, for example.

If you are using several effects in combination, the order in which they are connected has a considerable bearing on the eventual sound. For example, connecting in the order guitar-wah-fuzz-amplifier will produce the effect of a fuzzed wah-wah signal, whereas guitar-fuzz-wah-amplifier will give a wah-filtered fuzz signal, and the two things are quite different. So it is advisable to experiment a bit in this direction; you may be missing out on a sound that you've heard but couldn't play. But *please* don't write to the music papers saying: 'I use the same make of fuzz/wah/strings/nail varnish as X (hero) and can't get the same sound,' because even if you used X's gear down to the same plectrum you would still need to *be* X to get the same sound. Part of the delight of music is contained within the variety possible, so play YOU.

Keeping it simple

The heading here really speaks for itself: electronics are there to increase the flexibility and versatility of the instrument, but all too often they get in the way of the music. The fault lies not in the medium itself, which is obviously neutral, but in the approach of the player, or a misconception of what playing music *is* anyway. The ideal situation would be one in which the listener is not directly aware of the electronics at all, just the sound of the music; and the attainment of this ideal is all down to the expertise of the performer, his command and musical good taste. We do not imply that everything must be sickly-sweet and inoffensive; the most horrible sounds can often be in very good taste in a musical context. Think of the sound of the band as a whole, in which you and your instrument are a part; there should be spaces where your sound will fit, and you in turn should be leaving spaces for others. The simple, direct musical idea is often the most effective, projecting well within the larger context. This is not to say that the result should display a moronic monotony; the most complex forms may however be broken down into very simple components, each of which should be as perfect as possible when regarded in isolation. The player who devotes as much effort to a repetitive three-note riff as to the most complex passage, in terms of timing, texture and mood, is well on the road to the vital appreciation of simplicity.

Acoustics

In general terms, you are stuck with whatever acoustic properties the hall you are playing in possesses. You can only modify those properties in one of three ways: by physically moving the equipment or part of it to a different area of the hall; by altering the filter settings on the amplifiers or PA system, or by adding reverberation or echo treatments to part of the sound.

The actual moving of the playing position is of course likely to be impossible if there is a stage, and is really only practical

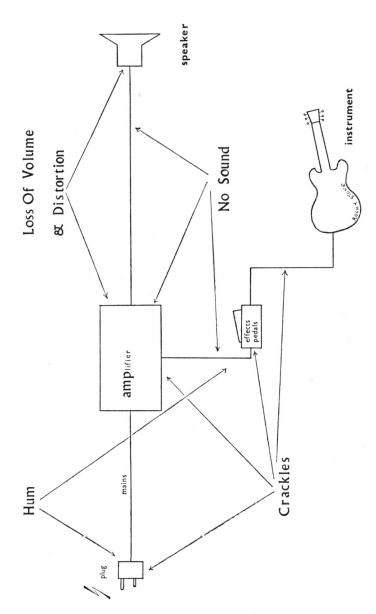

Loss Of Volume & Distortion

speaker

No Sound

instrument

Hum

mains

Crackles

plug

amplifier

effects pedals

Fig 27 Breakdowns

in lounge work. However, this does not usually preclude the movement of some of the speaker cabinets, and a few feet will often produce a surprising reduction in boom or unwanted resonance. Let us look at the various bad acoustic conditions which the band is likely to encounter, and discuss which of the methods listed above will be most effective.

Echo is usually immediately apparent on setting up, and although a moderate amount will impart a degree of 'life' to the sound, echo in excess will degrade the clarity of the music, muddying the percussion in particular. The cause is an over-reflective internal surface to the room, often a great bare wall directly opposite the stage. One simple move can often have a surprising effect: draw all the curtains. As the hall fills up echo will tend to diminish, the people themselves absorbing some of the sound. The use of echo and reverb effects on the amps should be reduced to a minimum in this sort of situation.

Boom or bass resonance is usually caused by a bad room shape, leading to easily induced standing waves, and there is little that can be done without rebuilding the hall. This condition will often produce excessive feedback on the PA and may not be apparent until playing is well under way. Moving the playing position to a different part of the hall can often help; if this is not possible, moving the bass enclosure and PA speakers to one side or forward should be tried instead. Roll off most of the bass boost on the amplifier tone filters.

Dead acoustics are usually found in lounges, hotel bars, etc; the exact opposite of the echo-prone hall, they are caused by an excess of soft furnishings and hangings, which absorb all the sound. As a result the music sounds flat and lifeless, and individual instruments thin and lacking in tone. A lively sound can be restored by the use of reverberation and echo effects on the vocals and solo lines. Opening the curtains to obtain a reflective surface will help.

The regular performer will also encounter all sorts of peculiar acoustic effects for which an obvious explanation is lacking;

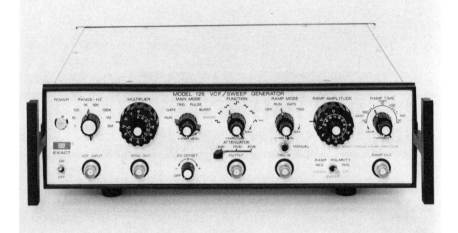

Page 101 (*above*) The Exact Model 126 Function Generator. A versatile, high-quality tone generator of lab. standard; (*below*) The Hammond Concorde: a good example of an organ incorporating both pre-sets and drawbars

Page 102 (*above*) The Sound City Jo'anna: an inexpensive electric piano that must be coupled to an amplifier and speaker system; (*below*) The Pianomate, seen here on the keyboard of an ordinary piano, adds organ-type tones via its own amplification system

some rooms are 'right', others do not suit a particular instrument. The answer lies probably in the individual frequency response of the particular venue; the guitarist may have a great sound and the drummer be struggling all night. If a room is not designed and acoustically treated specifically for music, then it is likely to be unsatisfactory for at least one player in the band.

Breakdowns

And what of those times when things go wrong, badly wrong, in the middle of your performance? Even the best maintained gear is apt to throw a nasty from time to time; standing there with lifeless guitar, feebly bleating that it's 'gone dead', puts the player in an unenviable position. Always carrying one spare general-purpose amplifier is a very good insurance policy for any band. Self-help is the best solution to minor faults; see the Smith & Jenkins fault-finding chart in fig 27, which should be memorised and then swallowed in the privacy of your own home.

No sound is the obvious fault to begin with. Assuming that all leads are connected, instrument to amplifier and amp to speaker, the next thing to assume is that there may be a fault in one of them, either at a jack-plug or in the form of an internal breakage. Check that the speaker is producing some noise, in the form of a gentle hiss; this will eliminate the speaker lead and let you know that the power stage of the amp is at least functioning. Check the instrument leads by substitution (always carry at least one spare) and take the effects boxes out of circuit in case the fault lies there. If all this fails, then the pre-amp must be dead – has the HT fuse blown? – and a spare must be substituted. Any failed leads or plugs should of course be a priority for repair *before* the next gig.

Crackles and *noises* will again be best eliminated by a deductive process. The obvious culprit will be the instrument lead or a socket in the instrument or one of the pedals. The mains plug can also produce noises if one of the wires is arcing

103

owing to a poor contact. If all this produces a negative result, then the amp must be at fault, or its fuse holder.

Loud hum will usually be traceable to an open circuit on the signal line, eg a lead out and lying on the floor or a plug shorting internally via a whisker of wire. More rarely it will have its cause in an earth loop (see Chapter 4) induced by an untried variation in the stage set-up, where amplifiers have been substituted following a previous fault.

Loss of volume and/or *distortion* can be laid at the door of the amplifier and will indicate an internal fault about which you can do nothing on the spot. More rarely, the speaker may be responsible for distortion as such, and that will require new drive units. It is possible for a faulty instrument lead to produce a loss of volume rather than an outright failure or nasty crackle.

Smoke from the amplifier means you've blown it, baby, the transformer, that is; so switch off quick and check your bank account.

Chapter 6

RECORDING

For centuries music, and its performance, has been an instantaneous experience, along with drama, differing in this respect from almost all other forms of creative endeavour. Music could only be heard as it was played, its boundaries of retention and recall limited and defined by the capacity of the brain or fossilised within a cryptic written page; the author's book could be picked up at will, a painting scrutinised for any length of time, but music vanished into the realm of memory as the performer laid down his bow. The transfer of this experience to permanent record, repeatable at will, demanded at first mechanical devices (wax cylinders, discs) and later electrical-mechanical (disc and amplifier involving a transducer) or more purely electromagnetic (magnetic tape); today, although the retail product in the form of a recorded work may be either a disc or tape (in cassette or cartridge form), all studio work involves firstly the production of a master magnetic tape, from which discs or tapes are manufactured.

Commercial recording studios vary in size and complexity according to their use, from large installations capable of housing a full symphony orchestra run by the large record companies and film studios to tiny cellar studios involved in the production of artist's demonstration tapes and TV jingles. The working musician will come into contact with recording studios in various contexts, and be expected to cope, and it is from this standpoint that we will approach the following survey. Recording artists are of course contracted to their record company for a specific period; they must turn out a certain quantity of material, which the company produces, packages and promotes. Profits will be shared on a royalty basis, as with books. For every band which has a record contract, however, there must be a hundred which do not and which are attempting to catch the ear of a company. One way of getting noticed is to produce a 'demo' (demonstration) tape or disc for audition, and this could place any band in the studio.

Recorded music of all types is in huge demand for TV and films, background muzak tapes for use in hotels and restaurants, backings for solo artists and cheap 'cover' versions of popular tunes. All this activity means a large demand for the session musician, who usually works for a fixed fee and with near office hours to be kept on a tight studio schedule. Once inside the studio, the musician is faced with a host of unfamiliar demands and pressures, the main one being the fact that time is cash, and a mistake or fluffed intro is not now something to be shrugged off, but represents £x; whether this is a desirable environment for creative endeavour is of course open to question. In an attempt to provide themselves with a less pressured environment, many musicians have set up their own studio at home, and this is a possibility which we shall discuss later in this chapter.

THE STUDIO

A commercial recording studio resembles a factory or workshop, in as much as it handles raw materials via production workers to complete a marketable product. In this case the raw materials are the musicians, their instruments and the sounds they produce; the production workers are represented by the engineer and producer, and the end product is a master tape, suited to the automated production of discs or tape cassettes for retail. Studio design should therefore be governed by considerations of efficiency for its appointed task, so as to ensure a consistent and repeatable quality in the end result. All the foregoing may seem somewhat alien to a creative area; however, an efficient approach to such a skilled operation can only be desirable, provided that quality and imagination are not made to suffer at the hands of economic necessity. Ideally, there should be an artist on both sides of the control room window.

For a general layout of the studio see fig 28. This area may be thought of as two distinct entities: the studio space for the musicians, and the control room for the electronic equipment and technicians. The control room is what we may term a 'concrete' area, where the equipment will be a permanent fixture, replaced only when an advance in audio technology dictates; the studio itself is a 'fluid' area, which has to accommodate many physically differing musical set-ups, and there are few fixtures. The first necessity is for total sound insulation between the two sections, to enable the engineer to judge the sound solely by that which is arriving electrically at his mixing desk, rather than what is being acoustically radiated. The walls (and windows) of the studio must be soundproof, not so much to prevent noise getting out, as to prevent extraneous noise getting in. The internal wall, ceiling and floor surfaces must be treated to minimise reflection and produce a 'dead' or non-reverberant acoustic environment. The smaller the studio, the greater will be the difficulty of obtaining good separation between the various instruments, particularly where amplification is involved; to overcome this, movable screens are used, and soundproof cubicles for the drums. In large studios this may not be necessary, sufficient distance achieving the same objective.

The performer's area will obviously vary in size, but it should provide for a minimum of five musicians and their equipment. Large unwieldy instruments such as pianos, percussion and speaker cabinets will be more or less permanent fixtures, situated where the engineer has found from experience that they record best. There will be monitor speakers for replay of tape to the

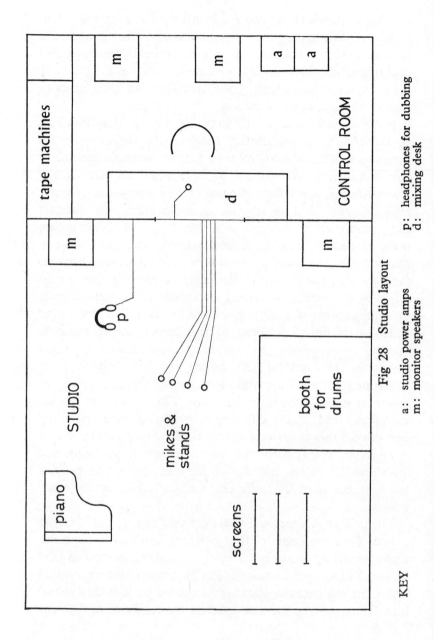

Fig 28 Studio layout

KEY

a: studio power amps   p: headphones for dubbing
m: monitor speakers   d: mixing desk

musicians, and to provide a communication channel from the control room; headphone outlets will be provided so that performers are able to hear backing tracks when overdubbing. There will also of course be a large number of microphones, stands, screens, and movable furniture. The arrangement of all these items will be determined by the engineer for specific jobs.

The control room will generally be much smaller than the studio. It is intended to house all items of recording equipment with the exception of the microphones, together with the engineers and producer; the nerve centre of the room is the mixing desk, into which all incoming signals are fed for the necessary balancing and filtering prior to their transfer to tape. There will be several tape machines, usually comprising a master multitrack machine and two or three variable track decks for copying and mixing down, depending on the systems in use; these will be linked back to the mixing desk and, via studio amplifiers, to monitor speakers.

These then represent our essential studio facilities. The functions of the producer/engineer team may be broadly clarified as follows, although they may at times overlap: the engineer has the job of getting the sound on to the tape at as high a quality as possible, of miking up and dealing with the mixing, dubbing and all technical problems. The producer's job is to direct the session in the broadest sense, forming a liaison between the wishes of the record company, the musicians and the engineer; he may advise and determine both musical and technical directions. Many bands these days produce themselves, and we are rapidly moving toward a time when electric musicians and composers will be equally at home in any part of the studio process.

MIKES AND MIXERS

Getting the sound on to the tape involves us with two elements; the microphone to convert the sound waves to an electrical signal, and the mixing desk with its filters and gain controls for the treatment of the signal before it is recorded. There are obvious similarities here with the miking up of a band through a large scale PA. Microphones for studio use will generally be ribbon, dynamic, or capacitor types (see p 18) depending on the specific application involved, which we will discuss later. Also needed will be a variety of stands to position the mikes firmly and accurately; system impedance for studio work will be 600ohms (balanced line), which allows the use of lengthy cables without loss of top frequencies. All mike lines will run back through the control room wall and into an input channel on the mixer. Basically, therefore, we have an acoustic sound source, a microphone positioned to pick it up and an incoming signal at the mixer, the quality of which will be determined by the capability of the mike and its position in relation to the source.

The studio mixing desk performs the same basic function as all the other mixers we have so far discussed; it combines, balances and filters a number of incoming signals to create a unified output. This type of mixer is, however, subject to increased demands of quality and capability. First, it must add no extraneous noise to the signal from its own circuitry; in practice, this can never be wholly avoided but is reduced to the point of inaudibility. Noise levels of this kind are measured and compared by signal-to-noise ratios, and expressed in terms of decibels below output level (see Appendix, p 149). Secondly, the number of input channels available will be very large (thirty or more is common) and the filter and gain facilities on each will be very comprehensive; besides the usual treble and bass filters there should be a number of additional treatments, which we will examine more fully at the end of this section. Fig 29, which illustrates multitrack mixing processes, represents in schematic form the basic signal path through the desk, which for the sake of simplicity is linked to a four track tape machine; this should not be confused with domestic four track recorders, on which only one or two (for stereo) tracks can be recorded

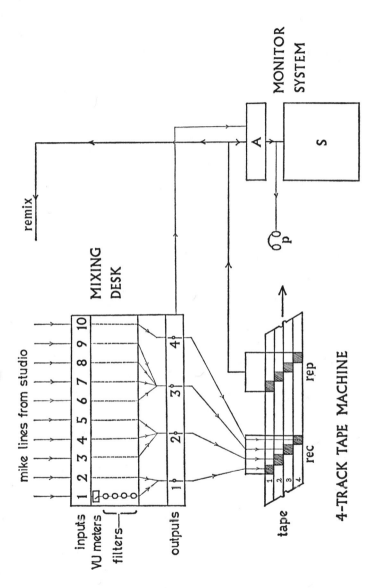

Fig 29 Multitrack recording

KEY
A: amplifier

p: studio headphones
S: monitor speaker

rec: record head
rep: replay head

or played back simultaneously. On studio machines all tracks can be recorded or played back simultaneously, and up to forty tracks are now possible; sixteen tracks are usual these days. The plate on p 52 shows a typical multichannel mixing desk. In fig 29 it will be noted that the inputs at the mixer can be linked to any of the four outputs, either singly or in combination; thus we can mix down the signals from mikes 1 and 2 to a single output 1 on to track 1 of the tape. Other mike inputs, 3, 4 and 5, can be mixed via output 2 to the tape on track 2 and so on; in general each track will represent the signal from one instrument or group of instruments, and the result will be a multitrack master tape. One essential for the engineer is some form of monitoring, via lab-standard amps and high grade speakers; the signal may be monitored from the mixer before it goes to the tape, and as a check on recorded quality it will also be monitored off the tape via the replay head. This system is known as A/B monitoring.

We now have a multitrack tape. Each instrument or group of instruments occupies one track and is individually balanced for an optimum dynamic level, but the tracks are unbalanced against each other. The next step must be to produce an overall balance on two tracks for stereo, and this involves the second stage of the process, mixing down from the tape. The recorded signals are taken back to the mixer inputs from the replay head, remixed and balanced to two channels. A high grade two track machine will be used for this final mix, and the resulting tape used in the production of discs, cassettes and cartridges or broadcasts.

Mixers for studio use are built to order and to suit individual requirements; this is made possible by modular construction methods, where the control circuit for an individual channel plugs in to the board. A typical desk will have a great number of sophisticated facilities of which we will mention a few. *Panning controls* enable signals to be 'leaked' into other channels to produce a stereo image. There will be *echo link* facilities so that reverb and delayed echo may be added to the mix from

112

external plates and tape delay units (see Chapter 3, p 67 for an explanation of these treatments). *Compressors* limit the dynamic range or amplitude of the signal to a previously determined level and remove the possibility of inadvertent tape overload. New developments in the field of mixing are centred on the use of computerised circuits, including memory devices which can repeat a given mix or perform many of the purely automatic monitoring functions for level etc; possibilities here include the freeing of the engineer for a more creative role generally. The studio mixing desk is the heart of the whole recording process, and we have really only touched the surface of the subject.

TAPE MACHINES

The reader will by now have dimly realised that studio tape machines are likely to bear little resemblance to the one Grannie uses for recording her budgie. They certainly look different, although the basic principle involved is the same; as we have put all our mixing and monitoring functions elsewhere, there is no need for the expected bunch of knobs, dials and flashing lights. Essential are the following requirements. (a) Perfect tape transport. Speed must not deviate either in slow movements up and down (*wow*) or in fast fluctuations (*flutter*). Both of these cause changes of pitch on the tape, and can be especially noticeable on instruments like the piano, rich in harmonics. (b) Wide frequency response. This should be in excess of the audible range, to allow for losses in later mixing; usual is from 20Hz to 30,000Hz. To achieve this, the tape must be transported at a relatively high speed, 15 or 30in per second. (c) Low noise. The machine should add as little noise as possible of its own in the form of hiss; this is especially important on multi-track machines, where we can end up with 32 tracks of hiss to mix down.

A few other physical features go along with the above, such as large reels to give a reasonable running time and wide tape on multitrack machines. Common tape widths are ¼in, ½in, 1in and 2in. A reel of 2in tape is very expensive.

ELECTRIC INSTRUMENTS IN THE STUDIO

Moving now from the technical victories in the control room, we are confronted with a situation in the studio itself, which is far less predictable or controllable in absolute terms; for here we actually have human beings, renowned for their temperamental attitudes, playing weird and antiquated pieces of wood and brass and even growling or shrieking into our beautiful flat-response minimum-distortion microphones. The all-electric rock band is likely to be even more repulsive, as they drag into the studio a mountain of huge amplifiers distinguished only by the obsolescence of their circuitry, humming, crackling and hissing at a volume sufficient to give the engineer incurable tea addiction.

Electric instruments and amplifiers in the studio must be as noise-free as reasonably possible and small amps of high quality are to be preferred; remember, too, that a lot of noise can stem from faulty leads, sockets, and effects pedals. All this sort of thing should have been checked *before* going into a session, by you or the roadie. Fortunately two things tend to work for us: if we are playing at a low level, hiss will tend to be reduced, and if the levels are very high the sheer volume will mask it all out anyway, as it does on stage. The real problem occurs if there is a wide dynamic range involved in the music. Very loud bands will tend to give the engineer troubles, since good separation will be made difficult, particularly in a small studio, and a combination of close miking and screening must be used; turning everything down is no answer, as the musicians will be relying on a fairly high level for effects of tone and sustain. Vocals are usually recorded direct to the desk and the simplest way of handling this is to produce an instrumental backing track, dubbing the voice on a later take. When this is not desirable, due to the loose structure of the music or the desire

114

for a 'live' feeling, vocals will be close-miked and folded back to the performers via headphones.

The alternative way of handling electric instruments is to feed all or part of the signal direct to the desk. This takes control of tone etc out of the hands of the player, of course, and is really only useful when complete clarity and control are essential. It is a technique frequently resorted to with bass guitar in an attempt to get clarity at the bottom end of the sound.

ACOUSTIC INSTRUMENTS IN THE STUDIO

Acoustic instruments may not hiss and hum, but they present other problems and can very quickly show up weaknesses in the recording equipment. Generally speaking, they will have a very wide dynamic range, making it difficult to establish an optimum level, and in many cases a very wide harmonic range too. These problems are alleviated when we are using fairly distant mikes to pick up an overall balance from an orchestra or group of players, but become pronounced in close miking and soloist situations.

Acoustic players can move the sound source around relative to the mike, whereas a mike positioned in front of an amp is going to remain at that optimum distance no matter what the player does. If the sax player is weaving a bit on his feet, the sound will be peaking up and down in level as the instrument varies in distance from the mike, and the tone will be changing too. Breath noise from wind instruments can be another annoyance, usually overcome by distance or by pop filters on the mike; a similar problem comes from the finger squeaks from acoustic guitarists, which are usually left in.

MIKING UP

There are two basic approaches to miking up, which are indicative of different recording philosophies. The best way of explaining this is diagrammatically, so take a look at fig 30. A, B and C represent the first approach to miking, involving

115

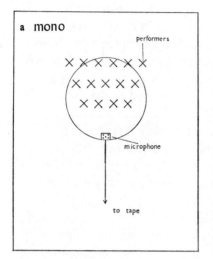

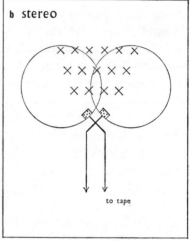

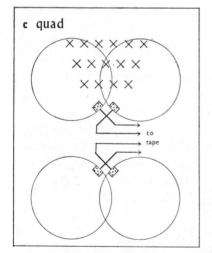

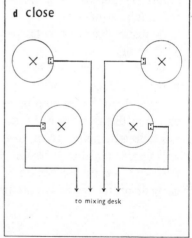

Fig 30   Microphone techniques

a natural balance from a group of players. The idea is that the finished recording should present the listener with a more or less exact reproduction of the sound he would hear had he been sitting in the concert hall or studio; all the parts will be performed simultaneously and the engineer's job is to get the sound on to the tape at an overall level. This sort of technique is losing ground a little, owing to the difficulties of overall control, and is generally restricted to the recording of classical and orchestral music.

The three variations shown represent an evolving technique of realism on the final product; A is the straightforward *mono* set-up, where one high grade mike takes the natural balance of the band back to a single channel. B shows the textbook set-up for *stereo*, where we have two mikes close together and angled at 90° to each other (known as the Blumlein technique after the man who thought it all up). Here, players on the left will record most strongly on the left-hand mike, and thus appear on the left-hand speaker eventually, whereas players stage centre will record equally on BOTH mikes and thus appear central on playback. This is the basis of a natural stereo image, and gives the music a lateral dimension in the forward plane. Two discrete channels must be provided throughout the recording process.

When a listener is sitting in the concert hall, not all the sound reaching his ears is being directly radiated from the players; the total ambience or acoustic is made up of the reflected sound reaching his ears via the back of the hall, ceiling etc. In an effort to reproduce this total ambience, sound engineers have gone one better than stereo, an advance requiring four discrete channels throughout the audio chain, known as *quad*; we show the set up in C. Four mikes are needed, two pointing forward as for stereo and two backwards to pick up reflections. The result, when played back over four speakers, more nearly represents a live acoustic. All these set-ups demand the use of identical, matched mikes.

D represents the alternative of close-miking, now almost universal in recording electric music. The essential point to grasp is that this technique can produce any of the effects mentioned above – stereo, quad, reverb, ambience etc – via the mixing desk. There need be no balance as such between the instruments in the studio, since players can hear each other via headphones, and each instrument can be individually recorded at its optimum level; the mikes used can vary widely in type and frequency response, but should usually be highly directional in polar response to avoid overspill from the other instruments. Many recording jobs will utilise a combination of methods to suit a particular requirement. Close miking puts the balance and eventual musical effect in the hands of the engineer, who therefore assumes an important creative responsibility.

We cannot delve fully into all the ramifications of miking up individual instruments, which could easily occupy a book in themselves; we will confine our treatment to a few basic ideas, useful to those contemplating a home studio or involved in taping their music on an amateur level.

Amps: cardioid mike close in, aligned on speaker axis. With bass guitars very high sound pressures are involved, so the mike should be a robust moving coil type with good low frequency response; ordinary vocal mikes are useless for this, since they have a built-in bass cut to reduce feedback.

Drums: ideal is one cardioid mike for each individual drum, placed to one side of the top head, close in. A good omni-directional mike slung some 2–3ft above will take care of the cymbals.

Piano: on a grand with the top off, a ribbon mike suspended one foot above the treble end of the frame; on uprights, omni-directional mike at shoulder height, about two thirds of the way toward the treble at the back.

String bass: small dynamic mike, wrapped in foam and pushed into the lower scroll of one of the *f* holes.

Page 119 (above) Three popular effects boxes – tone generator (Banshee), fuzz box and ring modulator; (below) The authors in their small electronic music studio – John is adjusting the keyboard

Page 120 The EMS Synthi-A synthesiser: the programme shown in figs 7–10 is set up here on this portable, low-price synthesiser

All these are suggestions only; there are many ways to mike up, all giving slightly different effects, and everyone has their pet methods. In the studio, of course, it's all down to the engineer; and if he doesn't know more than you do, what are you doing there anyhow?

DUBBING AND MIXING

As we have seen, there are two concepts or recording, which can be summarised under the headings of natural balance and synthetic balance. This section deals with the techniques of synthetic balance. Using close miking, as in fig 30 (d), we can balance a number of instruments in the studio to an overall level from the mixing desk, feeding the end result to one track for, say, mono. If we have panning facilities on the desk, we can divide each signal up into right and left channels and mix down into two tracks for stereo reproduction. With no more than two tracks available, the only way to add vocals or solos on a separate take (which as we have seen, may often be desirable) is to over-record or dub on to our existing tape. This is most easily accomplished using two tape recorders. It has a number of disadvantages; the quality of the original track will tend to be degraded, and hiss and tape noise will build up to an unacceptable degree. In fact, we won't manage more than around three dubs with a small home machine, and probably only six or so even with a Revox. There is another limitation involved when we have only two tracks available; the mixing process is very much a 'one shot' affair, and if it is not right there is no option but to play the music all over again.

The answer to this time-wasting dilemma is multitrack, and almost all modern studios will have more than four recording channels available. With sixteen or thirty-two tracks, each individual instrument will have its own path on the tape, placing actual mixing as a secondary process which can be repeated as many times as necessary, even after the musicians have gone home. In most situations we are also going to have quite a few tracks to spare, so over dubs are now made easy; there will be no degradation of the original signal, as the dubs can have a channel all to themselves.

Overdubbing and layering involve us with a number of interesting concepts. Recording a large-scale work, there is no need to have all the musicians in the studio at the same time; the violinists, for example, might never meet the horn section, as their recording date could be on a different day.

This removes the obstacle of insufficient space for large numbers of players in the smaller studio. One musician can, by layering several tracks with different instruments, build up a complex recording on which he plays guitar, bass, piano, and saxophone all at once. Many bands use this technique to increase the range of instrumental textures available to them. Old recordings can be updated by having new backings and arrangements added to the original material; in one authenticated instance, the live recording of a band's concert was so heavily remixed and dubbed that the only part of the original remaining on the final LP was the audience applause. Another advantage is the easy eradication of mistakes. If the guitarist fluffs his solo it can simply be re-recorded without disturbing the rest of the original take. Ally all these possible uses of tape to a synthesiser, and we have a uniquely flexible instrument for the composition of pure electronic music, which we will examine more closely later.

With multitrack recording we still have a problem with tape hiss, as each track will have some unwanted noise, no matter how good the machine; and this noise multiplied by a factor of, say, 32 can present problems. One solution is selective boosting of the signals most affected by hiss (ie low level, high frequency) above their normal amplitude on their way through the desk; they will then be comfortably above any noise on the tape, but out of their true dynamic range. They must then be reprocessed on playback, to take them down in level to their original position, the hiss being automatically reduced at the same time. This

122

system is known as the *Dolby* process, and there are variations for professional and domestic use. Many high quality tape machines for the home will have a Dolby processor built in, and its use is almost universal on stereo cassette decks.

Assuming a high quality on our original tape, mixing is the most important and individualistic operation of the whole recording process. In the production of an LP, the most important contribution to the eventual sound after the musicians themselves will be the mix; and no two producers will have the same concept of the ultimate treatment.

DEMO TAPES AND DISCS

Bands, groups and solo artists all make demos; so they must need them. Or, to be more exact, the record companies, producers, agents and all the people involved in the music industry must need them; the band doesn't, they already know what they sound like – or so they fondly imagine. The demo is in effect the band's shop window, in which it must display its capabilities to the very best advantage; and so the demo must be the very best you can do, recorded in the best possible way. This rules out straight away any ideas of doing a demo at home with ordinary domestic machines, since by making the man listen to a distorted, messy, hiss-laden tape you are killing your chances from the start. Demos *can* be done at home or whatever, but you will need good gear and a fair bit of know-how; seeing that in any case you would be unlikely to equal studio quality, the chances of your getting noticed are likely to be correspondingly reduced. Tape standards for demo purposes obviously don't have to be up to LP masters, of course, but good balance and the facility for dubbing are essential; those lucky enough to have a home studio with a small desk could probably do an acceptable job.

So our demo should be made in a professional studio, and the choice of which one is all yours. Costs will vary enormously, as will facilities offered; and there is really no substitute for personal knowledge or expert recommendation. Periodicals such as *Melody Maker* or *Studio Sound* often run features on this type of studio, and the adverts in the back of *MM* in particular are a mine of information. Unless your band is very large, you won't really want more than four track for a demo; spend your money on a good engineer and mixing rather than multiple track facilities. Make sure you choose a studio familiar with the special techniques required with electric bands and your type of music; this is especially important outside London, where small studios may rarely handle this type of work.

Assuming that the studio is going to get your sound on to the tape and produce a good mix, the next point to consider is your end of the job. *There must be no rehearsal in the studio.* All your musical worries with whatever number(s) you are recording should have been sorted out in rehearsal before you set foot in the studio, and the band should know their stuff backwards. Remember too that you are recording, not performing, and you should have practised doing just that; if there are vocals involved, they will be dubbed on separately, so you should practise playing the backing on its own, and the singers should practise over the backing track via headphones if you have a tape machine.

If this is your first time in a studio, and for many bands a demo often is, the following points could be helpful. Obviously, get to the studio and get set up in good time; many studios will give you about fifteen minutes free time for this, and you can cut down further by utilising a studio which has amps, drums etc already available. Do what the engineer says, with regard to positioning the gear, and let him get on with miking up and balancing your levels; in general follow his instructions with regard to levels etc, and if for some good reason you can't, explain why. The engineer will make it his business to understand the structure of the music, length of backing, number of vocals and extra solos, and should explain what facility he has for adding echo and other effects. If he doesn't, start worrying. A producer, preferably someone who already knows his way

124

around not only the studio but your music, is worth his weight in gold. After the session, you should have included in your costs about another hour for mixing down and copying; you should walk out with the multitrack master (you paid for it) and one or two mixed copies at $7\frac{1}{2}$ips. Discs can be pressed for you from these, but the cost is high and hardly repaid in terms of convenience.

All right, so now you're looking for a record contract. This means that your demo must be heard by a record company, via their A and R man (artists and repertoire), who auditions your tape and tells you if it stinks or otherwise. First off: there is no point in taking around even the very best tape if your band is not a working one. Record companies like to know that you are playing regular gigs and are popular, and will probably want to see you playing live if they are at all interested. Secondly, you should have a *manager*, if only a token one, and be able to refer the company to him for the business aspect of things; that way it looks as if someone at least is interested in you as a commercial proposition. The addresses and phone numbers of the various companies you can get from the Yellow Pages; always make an appointment to see the person you want. There is no point in posting tapes or leaving them in the office: they won't get heard. Be a real nuisance if you have to, but make sure you sit down with the A and R man and listen to it on the spot.

If after all this you are lucky enough to arouse someone's interest, you will usually be asked to make a test recording in the company's own studio. Depending on the result of this super-demo, you might even end up with a record contract.

HOME STUDIOS

If you have a suitable room for a studio, your horizons can be as wide as your pocket will allow. We must emphasise that anything approaching a professional sound will need an awful lot of money, and is hardly justified unless you can foresee a commercial return on your outlay; but for the purposes of rehearsal, composition and trial of ideas, a quite modest set-up will suffice. Assuming that this is your angle, we will examine some possibilities.

The basic room will mostly be a matter of what you can get. Rule out anything smaller than 16×12ft, or anything with high ceilings. Square rooms should be avoided, or any other shape which is boomy; cellar rooms tend to be prone to this, but will leak less noise to the outer world. Soundproofing is tricky, and there is no cheap and easy answer. Sound should not leak out to the annoyance of other inmates of the house and neighbours, and the acoustics of the room should be as dead (ie non-reverberant) as possible. One good method is to layer fibreglass wool over the walls and ceiling to a depth of about one inch, holding it in place with hessian or similar material; floors should be deep-carpeted with an underlay. If this is done thoroughly, there will probably be little need for additional foam wedges and so on inside. Leakage around and through doors and windows is always the biggest problem: the best way with windows is simply to block them off, or at least double-glaze with a 6in air-space. Doors, or a door, you have to have; ideal is a double door arrangement, but you will need a fair wall thickness for this, and a system of layering up the existing door may be more practical. Use $\frac{3}{4}$in chipboard on the outside, and a sandwich of softboard and expanded polystyrene on the inside, with a sheet of light alloy to reflect the treble; this will of course entail re-hanging the door and making a good seal round the edges with soft rubber strip. If you have problems with the sound going down through the floor, or up via the ceiling, you will have to lift the floorboards, pack in between the joists with fibreglass, and lay thick softboard on top of the original floor. And if the neighbours still complain? The legal position in the UK is that creating a nuisance of this type usually comes under a local byelaw, and before you can actually be prosecuted three separate householders must make a written complaint; however, you will usually be warned by the police before it gets to this stage.

Obviously it makes sense to utilise what you can of the gear you already use on stage, so we will assume that you already possess a good selection of microphones, stands and so forth. Later you will want to purchase high grade mikes specifically for recording, and a look at the catalogues will give you some ideas. The arrangement of the studio should follow the general principles outlined in Chapter 6; if you can't manage a control room, part of the studio should be set aside for the recording gear. Moveable screens will be useful, as your room is likely to be small. The tape machine(s) is very much a matter of what you can afford; it should have at least two channels (stereo) and A/B monitoring, which means three tape heads. Essential facilities on the machine are line inputs and outputs, VU meters for each channel, and a good general specification. Well-known machines in this field are the Revox and the Ferrograph range. One stage more advanced is the four-channel recorder by Teac illustrated in plate on p 51 and a lot more expensive.

If you are using more than two mikes you will need a mixer of some sort, and here again the possibilities are endless; please don't buy some cheap little box that merely adds hiss. We have looked at mixers already in some detail, and you should have a fairly good idea of the facilities you will need. Again it is possible to use the mixer from the band PA system, provided it is quiet. Your monitor system will probably be headphones at first, later progressing to a high-grade stereo amp and some classy speakers; don't bother trying to monitor via your band speaker cabs, it'll just depress you.

Finally, a word on the obvious but often neglected: if you have stopped the sound going out, you have probably also stopped the air getting in, so leave a little hole somewhere. Otherwise the mixture of tobacco smoke, beer fumes and smoking amplifiers may prove too much.

127

Chapter 7
ELECTRONIC MUSIC

Electronic music is not really that new. It was foreseen in the 1920s, and its realisation began in earnest about 1950. Today there are hundreds of studios, about 10,000 serious compositions and countless commercial ones.

There are many misconceptions about electronic music: some musicians sincerely believe that it is there to put them out of work. They quote as supporting evidence the famous 'switched on Bach' album produced by Walter Carlos in 1968, in which a Moog synthesiser and a multitrack tape recorder have been patiently used to recreate some of the conventional works of J. S. Bach. These musicians would find their fears unfounded by listening to 'Zero Time' by Tonto's Expanding Head Band in which a Series III Moog is used to create very unconventional music.

Some believe that electronic music is trying to be iconoclastic. Again, this is not so. An art form changes by evolution, not revolution.

Others believe that this new music is highly technical, very cold and therefore totally uncreative. Again, this is usually false; at least, it should be. The assumption that a sharp blade and tape instead of a reed and clarinet, a computer instead of manuscript paper, are somehow less creative is a misconception of what creativity is all about. Creativity is the original idea – how this is communicated to an audience is a matter of technique. If the original idea is bad BASIC, COBOL or FORTRAN and a bank of voltage controlled oscillators will do us no more good than clarinets and manuscript paper.

Some of the possibilities now open in this field include:

(a) You can use any sound you like – for example, a natural sound like a waterfall could be recorded and used. You are no longer limited to the conventional instruments of the orchestra.

(b) You as a composer create and control the actual sound material yourself, and you present it personally to the audience.

(c) You can compose and explore structures far too complex for human performers.

(d) Exactness of tone can be achieved by going back to physical first principles instead of having to use the tones of conventional instruments designed perhaps 300 years ago.

(e) You can pan sound from one channel to another, thus making the 'instrument' appear to move physically.

Two recent developments have been of considerable significance. The first was the production of high-quality tape recorders in the fifties, and in the mid-1960s we saw the use of keyboards to control certain electronic circuits by voltage (such as oscillators, filters and amplifiers), a set-up designed by Dr Robert A. Moog. It is the combination of these two developments that has made possible the tremendous growth of interest recently in synthesisers.

SYNTHESISERS AND VOLTAGE CONTROL

A collection of voltage controlled electronic circuits (such as oscillators, filters and amplifiers) together with certain non-voltage controlled circuits (such as ring modulators and white noise generators) and a method of interconnection has come to be known as a *synthesiser*. In many ways this is an unfortunate name, since it implies that the device is used to synthesise or build up the sound of an instrument from its component harmonics. It can do this, of course, and it is used in this way by some composers who have a good multitrack tape recorder and plenty of patience, because a synthesiser normally produces only one note at a time. But rather than be purely imitative the synthesiser can be used – perhaps preferably – in uniquely original ways. As EMS put it . . . 'Think of a sound.' It is unlikely that our budding superstar let loose on a synthesiser for the first time would get any sound at all – it takes a lot of practice before you can 'think of a sound' and come near to achieving it.

We saw something of the voltage controlled oscillator (or VCO) in Chapter 1, in which the frequency generated and thus the pitch of the sound eventually produced can be controlled by applying a small DC voltage to an appropriate part of the VCO's circuit. Bob Moog and others have also published circuits for voltage controlled filters (or VCFs) and voltage controlled amplifiers (or VCAs). In the VCF the centre frequency of the pass band – assuming it is a band pass mode – can be moved up and down the audio spectrum by changing the small DC control voltage applied to the appropriate part of the VCF's circuit. In the VCA the voltage gain of the amplifier can be reduced (or the attenuation increased) by changing the amount of DC control voltage applied.

In fact, if we go back to Chapter 3, we will see listed there the treatments commonly found in any synthesiser – various filters, ring modulators, envelope modifier (or shaper) and reverb. Add to these various electronic sources (tone generators) with different wave forms, flexibility of inputs and outputs and – most important – a sensible method of interconnection or patching, put them all for convenience in one case, use voltage control wherever possible, and perhaps a keyboard, and you've got yourself a synthesiser. It is the use of *voltage control* that gives a totally new dimension to the whole concept.

The advantages include:

(a) One circuit can easily affect another circuit, the audio output from one becoming the control input for another. Look for example at fig 31. Here VCO_1 might be running at 300Hz and this passes through the VCA before reaching the output. If now VCO_2 is set to give a 10Hz small amplitude sine wave and this is used to control VCA, then the gain of

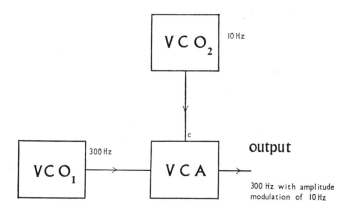

Fig 31   Application of tremolo

VCA will increase and decrease at a frequency of 10Hz. So the 300Hz signal passing through VCA will have its amplitude modulated at a rate of 10Hz. This is a tremolo treatment.

(b) Audio lines are electrically quite separate from control lines. Audio lines can therefore be kept quite short in length, reducing the risk of picking up hum and losing the treble. As an example consider fig 32. VCO is producing a triangular waveform which passes through the filter before reaching the output. Exactly which harmonics pass through the VCF depends on its response, and this can be set remotely from a considerable distance away by a pot and a $4\frac{1}{2}$V DC battery.

PROGRAMMING A SYNTHESISER

As this is not a manual for any one manufacturer we shall try and keep the discussion quite general in the hope that it will suit all readers, whatever machines they may have. To this end we shall use the block diagram approach. It is adequate for many purposes to classify the devices in a typical synthesiser

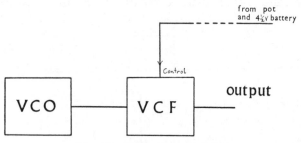

Fig 32   Remote control filter

in one of three ways – source, treatment and output device – and these are shown together with the symbols we have chosen to use in fig 33.

A *source* can be an electric signal generated from one of the special circuits in a synthesiser, such as an oscillator. Alternatives are a filter which can be superexcited and made to oscillate, and the trapezoid or outside shape of the envelope shaper. These are all probably voltage controlled, so we represent them by the left-hand symbol in fig 33 which clearly shows that the source has no input but consists solely of an output – the short line with an arrowhead on the right. The voltage control would be applied to the source, as shown by the inward arrow at the top of the

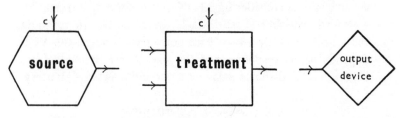

Fig 33 The symbols in use

132

symbol with the letter C beside it to indicate 'control'. The source *could* be external to the synthesiser. For example, you may wish to put a guitar through the synthesiser. Similarly the outputs from an organ, electric piano, microphone, or any bug for that matter, can be put through a synthesiser.

A treatment has one or more inputs and an output: examples are filters, envelope shapers, ring modulators, reverb and amplifiers, the majority of which are voltage controlled. The central symbol in fig 33 shows this.

The *output device* has an input only. It can be the monitor loudspeakers in the synthesiser, or a meter. It might lead to the external connection of power amplifiers and loudspeakers, tape recorders, other synthesisers and even light shows. The right-hand symbol in fig 33 shows this.

Now let's try putting it all together. In fig 34 we have a simple patch. The source is VCO$_2$ set to a 300Hz square wave,

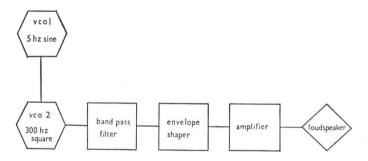

Fig 34   A simple patch

the output of which goes through three treatments – a filter set in the band pass mode, an envelope shaper, and an amplifier – and then to the output device which in this case is just a loudspeaker. The frequency of VCO$_2$ is controlled by VCO$_1$ which is set to a low amplitude 5Hz sine shape, and this has the effect of frequency modulating the 300Hz signal at 5Hz, or giving it a vibrato. It is not enough on any synthesiser simply to

133

patch the programme shown in fig 34. You will have to ensure that the control knobs for each of these devices are set correctly. In addition you may have to actuate the envelope shaper: on the EMS Synthi-A shown in plate on p 120 this is done by pressing the 'attack' button.

Suppose the envelope shaper is set on zero attack, zero on, slow decay and infinite off times (see fig 19). The sound you will hear then is the 300Hz signal, with a vibrato on it, smoothed in tone by the filter and decaying in volume once it starts.

But, we hear you saying, what's so special about this? And so far, of course, there is nothing very special about this. However, if you look at fig 35 you will see that it is precisely

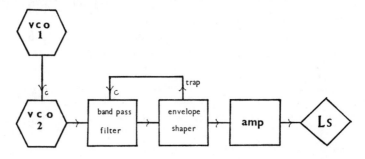

Fig 35   A better patch

the same as the patch in fig 34, except that we have added just one connection – the trapezoid output from the envelope shaper is now used to control the filter frequency. Now as the sound decays in volume its tone changes. Of course the source with this patch need not be an oscillator from within the synthesiser; a keyboard could be used instead, and this patch is then the one used quite a lot in 'pop' music.

Fig 36 shows a patch which, if set up carefully, can produce arpeggios or strange scales. VCO_2 needs to be set about 10 times higher in frequency than VCO_3, and with a smaller amplitude. Then, if the directions of the ramps are opposite, the resultant control voltage is of a staircase shape and as this is controlling VCO₁, the frequency of VCO₁, which was set to 300Hz, will in fact change by abrupt steps, and the series of notes produced form an arpeggio or strange scale.

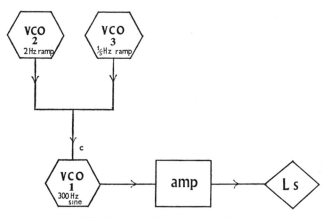

Fig 36   Producing arpeggios

Fig 37 shows a patch using the ring modulator to simulate bell or gong sounds. Both oscillators are set fairly high in pitch, one being sine shape and the other ramp or triangle shape. The ring modulated output is filtered to reduce the higher overtones. Note that a bell sound contains overtones which are not necessarily harmonics (or simple integral multiples of a fundamental) and consequently a ring modulator must be used if there is to be any hope of successfully synthesising the true sound.

Fig 38 is a more advanced patch capable of creating snare drum sounds, with a vague musical tone associated with each percussive noise. VCO_1 is the tone of about 120Hz which is abruptly ring modulated by the square wave from VCO_2 running at about 1Hz, and this is itself voltage controlled by the square wave from VCO_3 running at about $\frac{1}{2}$Hz. Both VCO_2 and VCO_3 are controlled by a joy stick – if you have one; these are handy

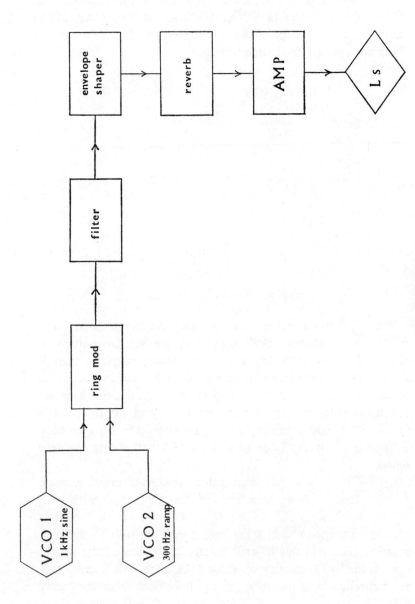

Fig 37   Simulating bell sounds

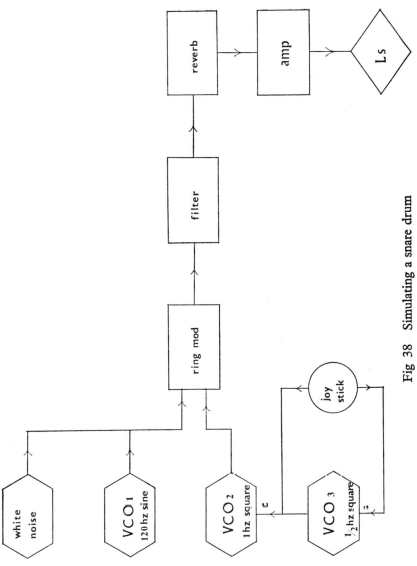

Fig 38   Simulating a snare drum

devices because they enable two parameters to be controlled by one hand. A white-noise generator is connected in parallel with the VCO$_1$ output, and this gives the necessary hiss sound. The

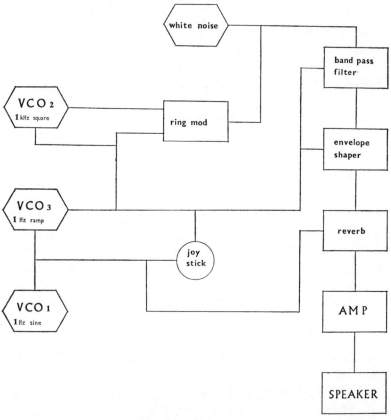

Fig 39   Space war

output passes through a high frequency band pass filter, and some reverb is added to give it a sense of space.

Fig 39 is our last patch, and the most complicated so far. We call it 'space war'. The main source of sound is a mixture of white noise and the output of the ring modulator, and this passes through the usual treatments. But these treatments are controlled, as are the inputs to the ring modulator, in a complex way. The envelope shaper is set on zero attack, zero on, slow decay, and automatic repeat. For an even more spectacular effect use the trapezoid output from the envelope shaper to control all the treatments and oscillators.

There are, of course, countless possibilities. There is nothing like experience. It is up to you to familiarise yourself with whichever synthesiser you have managed to get your hands on. Do read the manufacturer's manual carefully. Treat the synthesiser as if it were a very delicate piece of high class electronic sophistication, because that is just what it is. And have fun – maybe you'll find tomorrow's sound.

THE 'NO SOUND' SYNDROME

As Stravinsky said – 'the most nearly perfect musical machine, a Stradivarius or an electronic synthesiser.' But there is one very crude difference. If you cannot seem to get much sound out of the Strad you can always bow or pluck it harder. You cannot 'pluck' a synthesiser harder. If it is not programmed correctly in the first place no amount of excitation will help.

If you patch up a programme and there is no sound, check these points:

(a) The synthesiser is switched on.

(b) At least one source is patched through to the output, and is not subsonic or ultrasonic.

(c) All levels on the devices used are set above zero.

(d) The internal speakers (if these are what you are using) are not muted.

(e) The envelope shaper (if used) may need its 'attack' mode initiating.

(f) A white-noise generator (if thermionic) may need 30 seconds to warm up.

(g) The output amplifiers may have so large a control voltage applied to them that they are switched 'off'.

139

(h) Recheck that the programme is correct, that the devices are interconnected correctly and in the right order, and there is no electrical fault in the interconnections. (Do this by substitution.)

(i) Trace the source through to isolate where the fault is, by patching the signal to the output amp stage by stage through your programme, or patch to a meter if you have one.

(j) Think what you are doing. Read the section on programming again.

COMMERCIAL SYNTHESISERS

These were pioneered in the USA by Robert A. Moog, who was born in New York City in 1934 and took a PhD in engineering physics at Cornell University. His surname has become as synonymous with the synthesiser as has Hoover with the vacuum cleaner. Then there are ARPs from the USA and, in the UK, Dr Peter Zinovieff with his company EMS could well be the technical leaders at the moment. And there are others. The situation too is quite fluid. Since the subject is a fairly young one, each company is constantly improving the models in its range producing new versions which are more portable, more easily patched, more versatile and with more stable oscillators (so that they stay in tune better). All we can do here really is take a brief look at the range available at the moment from the top three. Remember that imported synthesisers are usually dearer than those made in your own country.

Moog

There is now a whole range of Moogs from the Mini-Moog at about £700 to the 111c at about £4,500. Basically each Moog consists of a number of separate, replaceable units called 'modules', each of which is a compact solid state circuit on a printed circuit card, so that the module is stable and easily serviced.

The main studio Moogs are coded 1c, 11c, 111c, in increasing order of complexity. Portable versions are coded 1p, 11p, 111p.

140

Prices range from about £2,500 to £4,500. All use the patch-cord system to route audio, control, and timing signals between modules, and all incorporate a keyboard. The 1c is an instrument of limited complexity designed to satisfy the requirements of independent composers. It is particularly suitable for use in the teaching of electronic composition, and is an appropriate starting point in establishing a serious electronic music (or EM) studio. The 11c is a moderately priced middle synthesiser, suitable for use in an extensive course in electronic music composition techniques and as a generating and treatment facility in a good EM studio.

The 111c is the largest and most versatile of the studio model machines. It contains about forty modules, comes complete with over forty patchcords and weighs 175lb. The main console cabinet alone measures nearly 50in by 16in by 14in. The XII is the most compact of all the Moog modular systems, but still provides all the basic synthesiser functions. It comprises just two portable units – a case housing the modules, and a keyboard controller – and is suitable for the studio as well as the gigs.

The Sonic Six and Mini-Moog are very suitable for the travelling musician. Both are compact, reasonably priced small synthesisers incorporating all the basic usual synthesiser functions and with the advantage for speed that they can be interconnected module to module by a switching system without having to use cumbersome patchcords.

ARP
Another popular group of synthesisers originating from the USA is that from ARP Instruments Inc. Some of the advantages claimed are their reliability, portability and modern electronics such as digital ring modulators, sample and hold circuits, and phase locked oscillators which are virtually driftless. The range includes the 2600 which is a really professional portable synthesiser weighing about 60lb and costing about £1,300.

A fairly recent addition is the Odyssey at about half the price,

141

weighing 20lb and containing most of the functions of a studio version. Both can be used without patchcords.

The 2500 is the large one and incorporates second generation design and thinking, giving the serious musician all the possible facilities with the convenience of metric switch patching.

Perhaps mention should be made of a small one – the Pro Soloist. This is a self-contained synthesiser using presets which can be placed on the top of an organ, for example, and gives 30 different instrumental voices; it has a touch-sensitive keyboard permitting the individuality of the musician to come through. By pressing harder on a key you can make the sound louder, brighter, add vibrato, even bend the note in pitch, or make it growl.

EMS

Electronic Music Studios of London, have a range of synthesisers and associated gear that many claim is technically superior to the American competition.

EMS have concentrated on voltage control and their first production in 1969 was a portable voltage-controlled studio with three oscillators known as the VCS 3. This has now been updated to a Mk II version which has a full complement of devices and treatments and is rigorously tested to a high laboratory standard specification. It costs about £400 without a keyboard. The Synthi-A, which is also now updated to a Mk II version, is a portable version of the VCS 3 in a smart attaché case but is not of the same laboratory standard. We have a close-up of this in plate on p 120. It is about £50 cheaper than a VCS 3.

With both the VCS 3 and the Synthi-A a keyboard is an optional – but very desirable – extra. The Synthi DK 1 keyboard will cost you another £150 or so, but is well worth it; it contains its own built-in oscillator and so produces a signal voltage and also a control voltage, depending on how fast a key is struck. This control voltage can be used to effect the volume of sound or the tone, or it can control the pitch of an oscillator back in the synthesiser so that this oscillator can, for example, be tuned a major third away from the keyboard and then automatically follow your melody line. The DK 1 can be seen in plate on p 119.

There are perhaps two major advantages with EMS equipment and both are concerned with programming a patch. Patching is by a 16×16 way-pin panel matrix completely eliminating patch cords. Each of the 256 locations in the matrix board can be designated by a map reference, and this is clearly shown in plate on p 120 which is the practical patching programme for fig 40. Let's check it out. Oscillator 1 output is on the

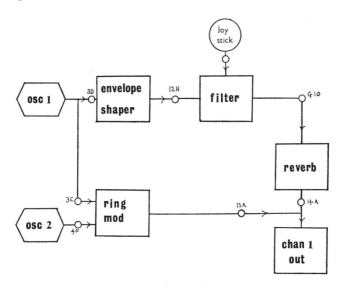

Fig 40   The patch shown in plate on p 120

horizontal line 3. So by inserting a pin at 3D we send this signal from oscillator 1 to the envelope shaper in column D. The output from the envelope shaper – called 'env signal' – is on line 12, but the input side of the filter is column H, so a pin at 12H sends the output of the envelope shaper into the filter. A pin at

143

10G sends the filter output into the reverb, and a pin at 14A patches the output of the reverb to the Channel 1 output. Oscillator 1 is set at a medium audio frequency to a mixture of sine and ramp waveforms. The filter is set to a sharply tuned position on the 'response' control and a low pitch on the 'frequency' control, the frequency being controlled by sideways motion of the stick because of the pin at 15N. The envelope shaper is set as shown and is not automatically re-cycling, so the 'attack' button will have to be pressed. The alternative signal line is oscillator 1 into Channel A of the ring modulator at 3E, and oscillator 2 into Channel B at 4F, with the output of the ring modulator continuously present in the Channel 1 output because of the pin at 13A.

The other advantage is a development of this. A printed circuit board of convenient rugged shape, called a 'Presto Patch', can be pushed into a special holder, thus taking the place of a particular programme of pins. This is clearly very fast, which is important when used live. EMS will even make up a Presto Patch to your own designs . . . at a cost of £10.

Don't forget that the sources and treatments have to be set correctly on their controls – it is *not* just a question of pushing a Presto Patch in.

Of course, EMS make more complex versions. The Synthi-AKS is a combination of the Synthi-A and another keyboard called a KS, which is touch-sensitive and incorporates a 128-event digital sequencer, which allows what has been played in to be recalled and altered. It comes in a strong lockable attaché case, weighs 25lb and costs about £450.

The Synthi-100 Professional Electronic Music Studio has probably the world's most comprehensive specification. It has as its heart a digital sequencer (which is a small special-purpose computer) complete with analogue-to-digital and digital-to-analogue converters. This device enables the operator to load, in his own time, up to six independent tracks of control voltage data, plus attack and switching pulses, then hear it played

144

back – forward or reverse – at any speed. And all events can be individually examined by stopping the clock, and edited or erased. It has two 60×60 pin panel matrices, one for signals and one for controls. It costs about £6,500. A slightly less complex studio, the Synthi-50, is available at about £1,000 less. The BBC Radiophonic Workshop is one of many famous institutions that have bought a Synthi-100.

EMS actually go even further; they will do a custom built complete computerised electronic music system at about £15,000.

THE ELECTRONIC MUSIC STUDIO

For the full realisation of electronic music a synthesiser is usually linked up with mixer, multitrack recorders, some non-VC devices and special indicators such as the cathode ray oscilloscope (CRO), which visually displays waveforms, and the digital frequency meter (DFM), which measures the frequency of the note and displays it as a precise numeral, so making the problem of 'tuning' a lot easier. The other main essential, assuming you have the gear, is patience . . . EM is a time consuming interest.

The smallest EM studio
Perhaps the smallest electronic music studio is shown in fig 41. All you need is a synthesiser and a stereo tape recorder . . . and imagination. You can record several sounds in succession and then edit the tape to make up a composition. Changing the speed of the tape recorder between recording and playback will change the pitch. The plate on p 119 shows the authors with an EMS Synthi-A, DK1 Keyboard, and some of the peripheral gear associated with their EM studio. Notice the CRO, DFM, Advance J2 tone generator, and Exact 126 function generator.

A more advanced studio
We conclude by indicating in fig 42 how a synthesiser could be connected to a large variety of peripheral gear by a patchfield,

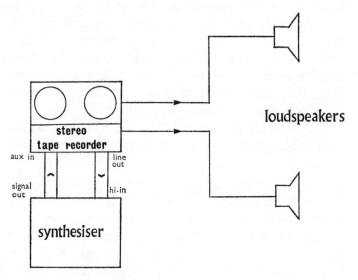

Fig 41   The smallest EM studio

which could be an EMS type 16×16 or 60×60 matrix.
As Francis Bacon put it over 300 years ago:

'Wee also have Sound-houses, where wee practise and demonstrate all Sounds, and their Generation. Wee have harmonies which you have not, of Quarter Sounds . . .'

Which is where we came in!

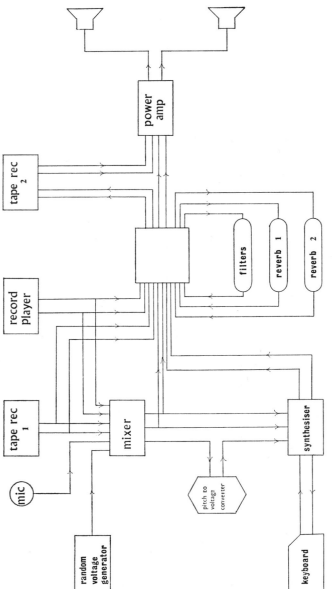

Fig 42 A more advanced studio

Appendix
THE PHYSICS OF SOUNDS

We conclude with a brief summary of the basic theoretical physics to which we have referred in the text.

Any sound is caused by a vibration and if the number of vibrations per second (or frequency) lies between about 20 and 20,000, then the sound is audible to the average person. The sound needs a medium in which to travel, and this is usually the air; sound will not travel through a vacuum. It travels with a speed of about 330m a second (say 1,100ft a second) through air at normal temperature, but faster if the air is warmer. It travels through the air as a longitudinal wave – the first molecule of air vibrates from side to side in the direction of the sound wave and vibrates the second molecule, which vibrates the third, and so on, and the sound wave shunts its way through the air in a similar way to an engine shunting trucks on the railway.

THE CHARACTERISTICS OF A SOUND
There are several characteristics of a sound and we will try to explain them here.

Amplitude
If we represent our sound wave by the sine curve of fig 43, which would represent the sound of a tuning fork, then the

maximum displacement of the air molecules is called the *amplitude* or peak value of the wave. It is the amplitude which governs the intensity of the sound wave, and it is this which produces a loudness to the listener. The actual loudness is of course

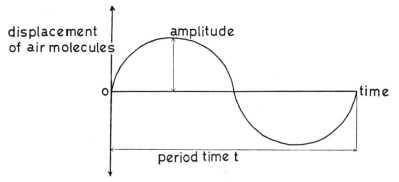

Fig 43   Characteristics of a sound wave

subjective – it depends on the person. A deaf person would never agree. Generally speaking, we can say that the larger the amplitude, the louder the sound.

The decibel or dB is now unfortunately being used as a direct unit of loudness, and there are venues where, if the relative sound intensity level at the monitoring point exceeds say, 93dB, then the electric mains supply to the stage cuts out for five seconds or so. All musicians should blacklist such pathetic misuses of electronics. The dB is a perfectly satisfactory unit for comparing one thing with another and you will find it used, not just in sound, but in electronics generally: the gain of an amplifier, the noise level of a mixer, the signal reduction by an attenuator, these can all be expressed in dB relative to something. But be careful. The dB is a strange beast. It is actually defined as ten times the logarithm to base 10 of the ratio of two intensities. This can give rise to strange things. For example, if an organist is playing at 60dB and a guitarist joins in and contributes another

60dB of sound, then the resultant sound intensity is now twice as high, or $10 \log_{10} (2/1)$ high or 3dB high. So 60dB added to 60dB makes 63dB.

Frequency

The second characteristic of a sound is its *frequency* or pitch, measured in the number of vibrations per second, now called Hertz or Hz. We give it the symbol f.

Look again at fig 43. The time of one complete wave is called the *periodic time* and given the symbol T. So if we have ten waves a second, each wave would take 1/10 of a second, and clearly f and T are the inverse of one another. As we said earlier, you cannot hear frequencies above about 20,000Hz. Dogs . . . and bats . . . can.

Harmonic content

The third characteristic of a sound wave is its *harmonic content*, which governs the tone or timbre you hear. A trumpet playing middle C with a certain loudness sounds different from a piano playing the same note with similar loudness, and this is mainly due to the fact that a trumpet's waveform contains a different harmonic content than a piano's waveform. Fig 44 shows the spectrum of a trumpet playing a note of frequency 175Hz. This shows that if an average trumpet is blown to produce a note of 175Hz, then in fact a whole series or spectrum of frequencies is produced. The first harmonic (175Hz) has an intensity of nearly 20dB, but the second harmonic of 350Hz has an intensity of nearly 30dB, whereas the third harmonic (525Hz) and the fourth harmonic (700Hz) are similar in intensity at about 17dB, and so on up through all the higher harmonics, which together give that particular make of trumpet fitted with a particular mouthpiece and blown by a particular person its own characteristic overall tone. And it could vary from one day to another owing to changes in temperature and humidity. The overall

150

shape of fig 44 could be quite different if our trumpeter blew a different note.

It is certainly different for a different instrument, and this is why we can tell one instrument from another by sound alone. It

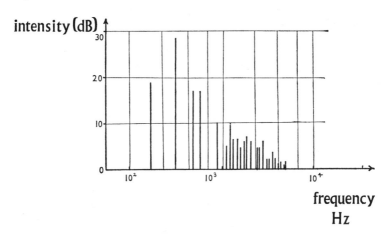

Fig 44 Harmonic content of a trumpet note

is said that for a stringed instrument the harmonic content even depends on the varnish used on the body of the instrument, so you can see that the business of tone is in fact a highly complex one.

Starting transient
The first few fractions of a second after a note is started can have a profound effect on the tone heard. Consider the difference between striking a note on a guitar with the finger and then with a plectrum. The difference in tone is due to the different pattern of harmonics produced as the note is started; after a fraction of a second these harmonics, which constitute the *starting transient*, fade quickly away and we then hear the normal tone of the instrument. Try an experiment for yourself. You need a good tape recording system and a piano. Record the melody

of 'God Save the Queen' (it *will* work for other tunes). Rewind, play it back, and you should have a perfect recording of the British national anthem. This was just to test that the recording gear was all right. Now record the same tune but, this time, play the tune backwards. Now if you simply rewound and replayed you would have the tune backwards, of course. But we are going to be a bit cleverer than this. Play the tape backwards. The tune comes out with the correct sequence of notes, but it sounds more like an organ playing 'God Save the Queen' than a piano. The reason is that the starting transients have artificially been put on the ends of the notes and are not occurring naturally at the start of the notes.

Envelope shaping
Envelope shaping in many ways incorporates the starting transient aspect. All sounds must grow in volume – we call this the *attack* – at a certain rate. They must stay *on* for a certain length of time. They must fade away – or *decay* – at a certain rate. Finally, they must stay *off* for a certain time. Fig 45 shows

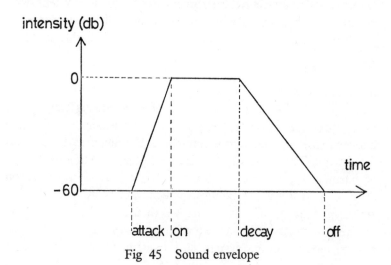

Fig 45   Sound envelope

152

the envelope of a certain sound: it has a fast attack, it remains on for a moment, then it slowly fades away with a fairly long decay, and finally it is off. The shape of the envelope is a trapezoid, and this is a very useful control voltage in a synthesiser. The shape of the envelope contributes significantly to the tone heard.

THE PROPERTIES OF A SOUND

Sound has many properties, most of which are common to wave motions generally. Light is a wave motion too, so it is not surprising to find that, just as light can be reflected, so can sound. In fact sound shares many similar properties with light. Apart from the fact that sound travels as a longitudinal wave through air molecules, and light (like radio waves) is a transverse electromagnetic wave, they also have one major point of difference. Sound waves travel about a million times slower than light waves: their wavelengths are very much longer and their frequencies very much smaller. This helps to explain why a light beam travels in a straight line with little dispersion, but a sound 'beam' does not. The shorter wavelength treble sounds tend to travel straighter than the long wavelength bass sounds, and this helps to explain why a PA column or a lead guitarist's stack points at the audience, whereas it does not really matter which way a bass stack is pointing.

Reflection

It follows that sound waves will reflect off surfaces. If the surface is hard and smooth, almost as much energy will bounce off the reflector as arrives at it. Fig 46(a) shows sound reflection in the ideal case of a directional sound beam, and fig 46(b) shows the more likely situation. It is quite clear then that any band playing in a hall with four vertical smooth walls and smooth horizontal floor and ceiling will have a severe case of the multiple reflections! Indeed, it is said of the Albert Hall in London that you hear the concert twice.

It could be worse. Fig 47 shows what happens if a beam of sound hits a curved smooth surface. Now the sound is focused to a point, marked F, where it will be unnaturally loud. This situation can occur in concert halls with curved ceilings.

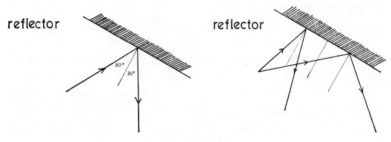

Fig 46   Reflection

Refraction
Just as light is bent or refracted in going from one substance to another – prisms and lenses are good illustrations – it is possible to bend sound waves by refraction. Sound lenses can be made (balloons filled with carbon dioxide are quite successful) but it is more usual to witness sound refraction due to wind and temperature gradients, and this can be of significance in large open-air concerts.

Interference
When a sound wave is reflected off a smooth source back on to itself, it will create regions where it adds and other regions where it subtracts. Where it adds – the antinodes – louder sound is heard, and where it subtracts – the nodes – you can have a region of no sound at all.

This also occurs whenever two sounds of the same amplitude and frequency meet; one does not have to be the reflection of the other. It is clear, then, that the space in front of the band's speakers is a complex interference pattern.

curved
reflector

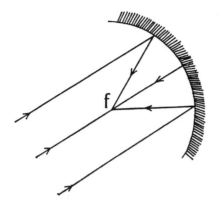

Fig 47   Focused reflection

Beats

Beats are a special case of interference. If a sound of frequency 300Hz meets another sound of frequency 302Hz, assuming their amplitudes are equal, then you hear the average frequency of 301Hz but its amplitude is changing twice a second. This is because the two sounds are beating together and the beat frequency is $302-300=2$Hz.

The good musician tunes by beats, because when zero beat is heard the two sounds have exactly the same pitch.

Diffraction

Light travels in straight lines, which explains the formation of shadows. But the wavelength of sound is some million times larger than light and consequently sound bends or diffracts around obstacles quite easily, making it impossible to find the 'shadow' of a sound. Loudspeaker horns make use of diffraction to increase their directional efficiency as the wavelength decreases.

THE VIBRATIONS OF STRINGS

Mersenne studied the vibration of strings as long ago as 1636. If a stretched string is plucked or bowed sideways in the usual way, a transverse wave travels in both directions along the string. When each wave hits the end, it bounces back; both reflected waves quickly meet and interference occurs. The result of this process is a collection of stationary or standing waves on the string. Fig 48 shows some of these, in increasing order of complexity. Do not forget that, in practice, a little of each of

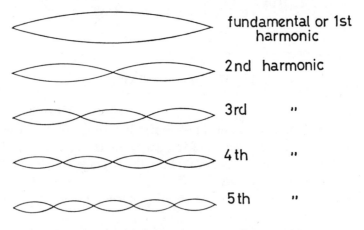

fundamental or 1st harmonic

2nd harmonic

3rd ,,

4th ,,

5th ,,

Fig 48   Vibrations of strings

these is always present. Indeed, in the case of a violin, there is still about one per cent of the energy in the seventeenth harmonic.

Suppose the string in question is a G string, perfectly in tune, on a guitar. The frequency of the G string will be 392Hz, (assuming we are tuning to A=440) so the first harmonic is 392, and the second harmonic will be 2×392=784 (which is an octave higher, G′). The amplitude of this second harmonic will probably be much less than that of the first, so it will appear quieter. The third harmonic will be $3 \times 392 = 1176$ which is the D above G', and it in turn will be quieter than the second harmonic. The fourth harmonic will be $4 \times 392 = 1568 = G''$, which is twice the second harmonic, so this one is two octaves higher than the first harmonic. The fifth harmonic is $5 \times 392 = 1960$ which is the B above G''. And so on.

The exact amplitudes of these harmonics, and consequently the tone of the resultant sound, depends primarily on the type or make of string and the guitar used, and the musician and where and how and with what he excites the string in the first place. If it is on electric guitar then the final sound heard will depend on the treatments and amplification used.

The velocity V of the sound in the string is related to the tension T and the mass per unit length m by this formula:

$$V = \sqrt{T/m}$$

and the frequency f of the note produced is related to V and the wavelength λ by this formula:

$$f = V/\lambda$$

Given that the frequency for the first harmonic is f_1 and the length of string $1 = \lambda/2$ then, by a little algebra juggling, we have this important formula for the frequency of the first harmonic:

$$f_1 = \frac{1}{2l}\sqrt{T/m}$$

Similarly, if the frequency of the second harmonic is f_2, we have:

$$f_2 = \frac{2}{2l}\sqrt{T/m}$$

and so on:

$$f_3 = \frac{3}{2l}\sqrt{T/m}$$

157

$$f_4 = \frac{4}{2l}\sqrt{T/m}$$

$$f_5 = \frac{5}{2l}\sqrt{T/m}$$

It follows that if the tension is higher the pitch of the note is higher; that if the length is shorter, the pitch is higher: and that if a lighter gauge of string is used the pitch is higher.

MODULATIONS

When a signal is changed or modified by a second signal we say that the first is *modulated* by the second. There are many ways of doing this, and – if you can face some trigonometry – we will look at three popular versions.

Amplitude modulation

This is the tremolo treatment and causes the amplitude of the signal – and consequently the eventual loudness – to change by about five per cent at a rate of between 5 and 10Hz in practice. Mathematically this is what is happening. If S is the amplitude of the signal of frequency f_s and s is its magnitude at a time t then :

$$s = S \sin (2\pi f_s t)$$

If M is the amplitude of the modulation of frequency f_m and m is its magnitude at a time t then :

$$m = M \sin (2\pi f_m t)$$

If now the signal is amplitude-modulated, the result is that the amplitude S of the signal is increased by an amount m so we have the result :

$$(S + m) \sin (2\pi f_s t)$$

which (we are sure you will agree!) can be written as :

$$S \sin (2\pi f_s t) + \tfrac{1}{2}M \cos [2\pi(f_s - f_m)t] - \tfrac{1}{2}M \cos [2\pi(f_s + f_m)t]$$

As we said earlier, S is usually much larger then M, and f_s much larger than f_m, so what this equation tells us is that we land up with (1) the original signal; (2) a smaller signal at a slightly lower frequency, and (3) another smaller signal at a slightly higher frequency. So we have introduced two new frequencies, one above and one below the original. These are called 'side bands'.

Frequency modulation
This is the vibrato treatment and causes the frequency of the signal – and consequently the musical pitch – to change by about 5 per cent at a rate of between 5 and 10Hz in practice – similar figures to those for the tremolo treatment.

The mathematics are quite frightening and we do not dare introduce them. Let us just record that the result $=$

$$S \sin [2\pi(f_s + m)t]$$

Ring modulation
This is a very unusual treatment and in many ways it is not musical at all. The ring modulator treatment actually multiplies the signal and the modulation together. So, assuming our signal is

$$s = S \sin (2\pi f_s t)$$

and the modulation is

$$m = M \sin (2\pi f_m t)$$

then if we ring-modulate s against m we get the result

$$= s \times m$$
$$= S \sin (2\pi f_s t) \times M \sin (2\pi f_m t)$$
$$= \tfrac{1}{2} SM \cos [2\pi(f_s - f_m)t] - \tfrac{1}{2} SM \cos [2\pi(f_s + f_m)t]$$

showing that the output contains two frequencies – one is the sum of the original frequencies and the other is the difference – but it does not contain either the original signal or the original modulation.

So, to put it quite simply, if a signal of frequency f_s is applied to one of the input sockets of a ring modulator, and a signal of frequency f_m is applied to the other input, then the output contains both $f_s + f_m$ and $f_s - f_m$ but neither f_s nor f_m. So the output can be musically unrelated to the inputs, which opens up interesting possibilities.

We will just mention here two particular uses of a ring modulator. Suppose the same signal is applied to both inputs, so that

$$f_s = f_m$$

Then the output must be $f_s + f_s$, and $f_s - f_s$. So the output is only $2f_s$ or one octave higher than the input.

Again, suppose the output is fed back as one of the inputs and f_s is the frequency of the signal applied to the other input, then the output frequency f_0 is $f_s + f_0$ and $f_s - f_0$.

$$\text{So } f_0 = f_s + f_0 \text{ which we ignore}$$
$$\text{or } f_0 = f_s - f_0$$

This gives us

$$2f_0 = f_s$$
$$f_0 = f_s/2$$

and the output frequency is now half the input frequency, or the output is an octave lower than the input.

The general point to remember with ring modulation, as we have tried to make clear in Chapter 3 is that if either or both of the inputs are not single frequency sine-curve waveforms, then they contain lots of harmonics. These harmonics all ring modulate against one another causing the outputs to be extremely complex. Remember there is no output from a ring modulator if there is only one input signal.

Finally, as a word of warning, do remember that with complex wave inputs some of the difference frequencies in the output can be very low indeed. So blow your mind and not your stack.

160

RESONANCE

There are many types of vibration possible – free, damped, natural and forced are all terms which you meet in the books. We will try and distinguish simply between these, and shed some light on one very important consequence . . . resonance.

Suppose you have a solid electric guitar and it is not connected to any amplification system. If you twang a string it vibrates freely. (Actually it is damped because the sound fades away.) The sound is not particularly loud. It would be louder if you tried this with an acoustic guitar, because the body of the guitar has a natural frequency at which it would prefer to vibrate and you are forcing the body to vibrate and this helps produce volume to the sound. The larger the body the lower its natural frequency, which helps to account for the size of a string double bass.

Fig 49 shows how the response of a body varies with the

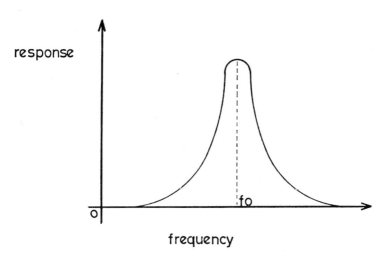

Fig 49   Resonance

frequency forcing it to vibrate. We see that, at both low frequencies and high frequencies, the response is poor. So somewhere in between there is a frequency f_o which gives a maximum response. This is the *resonance* condition. So if the forcing frequency happens to equal the natural frequency of the body, maximum sound is produced. Normally such resonances are avoided with acoustic instruments, otherwise – independent of the musician – some notes would be louder than others.

Resonances can occur on harmonics and might particularly be noticed if there is something loose.

Clearly, then, the natural frequency of the air column in a loudspeaker stack has got to be lower than any frequency you are likely to try and reproduce through that loudspeaker. So, as the volume of air is inversely proportional to the natural frequency, this accounts for the size of bass stacks!

You will also come across resonances in room acoustics, but you won't have much control over these.

INPUT AND OUTPUT IMPEDANCE

There is usually a considerable confusion in the minds of all budding superstars when it comes to the concepts of input and output impedance, and this is not helped by some of the advice given by the average music shop salesman.

In fig 50 we have represented the source of signal – say a

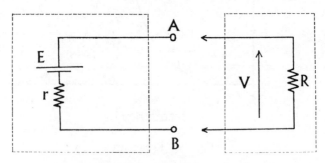

Fig 50 Input and output impedance: loads and sources

162

guitar, organ or tone generator – by a battery of voltage E and a resistance in series of value r. Terminals A and B are therefore the output terminals of the source – they could be the output jack socket connections on the guitar, for example. If we now looked into the terminals A and B with an impedance or resistance measurer, the amount we would see – the value r – would be the *output impedance* of the source. (Technically there is a difference between impedance and resistance – see below.)

Suppose now that the output at the terminals A and B feeds a load, such as the input of an amplifier. Then we can represent the input impedance of the amplifier by a resistance of value R, and suppose that the voltage developed across R is of value V. Let the current flowing be I. So E=V+Ir or, if you are good at algebra,

$$V/E = \frac{1}{1 + r/R}$$

The ratio V/E is the ratio of the useful output voltage V to the theoretically generated voltage E. Clearly we want V to be equal to E if at all possible. A little study of the above equation shows that this is only possible if r/R=0, which means that the output impedance r must be zero or the input impedance R must infinite. In fig 51 we have sketched V/E in percentage terms against the ratio r/R and this shows that we get 100 per cent voltage transfer from source to load only when r/R=0.

It is frequently said that 'the impedances must be matched', and this is frequently taken to mean that r=R. We see from fig 51 that, in this case, 50 per cent of the signal is lost. For proper matching it is essential that all output impedances are low, and all input impedances are high.

ELECTRICAL TERMS

We include here a brief summary of the most important electrical terms in use in the music business, without telling *too* many lies.

Have another glance at fig 50. Suppose it represents an amplifier on the left feeding a moving coil loudspeaker on the right. *Current* in amps will be flowing clockwise around the

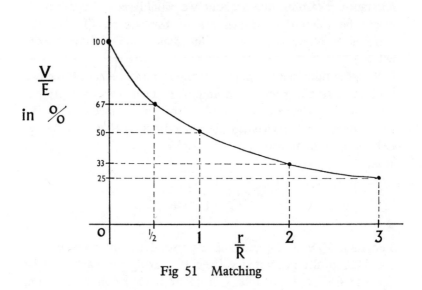

Fig 51   Matching

circuit and through the load resistance R (measured in ohms) causing a voltage or potential difference (PD) – which we measure in volts – across R. Perhaps the basic law in electricity is Ohm's law and this says effectively that:

$$\text{amps} = \frac{\text{volts}}{\text{ohms}}$$

Also, power (measured in watts) is dissipated in R, and

$$\text{watts} = \text{volts} \times \text{amps}$$

Suppose however that fig 50 represents a source on the left

164

feeding an amplifier on the right. Now R will be very large and the current flowing will be negligible, so the power transferred is negligible – it is voltage that is being transferred.

Resistance and *impedance* are both measured in ohms, but whereas the concept of impedance does not exist for DC (and all impedances behave like resistors) it must be used for AC and it then incorporates the resistance. Circuit elements like capacitors and coils have impedance but not resistance. Inside all amps you will find a maze of electronic components, a fair proportion of which will be *capacitors* (measured in farads). You might find an *inductor* – which is just a coil of wire – and is measured in henries. You will almost certainly find a complicated inductor with many coils wound on an iron core called a *transformer* and if this is a 'mains tranformer' it could be a 'step-down' one, meaning that it reduces the voltage. (Incidentally, that also means it increases the available current capacity.) On the front panel of most amps – disguised as volume or tone controls – you will find potentiometers or 'pots' and these can be physically circular or linear. Their variation of resistance with the amount of physical movement of the control knob can follow a log or linear law. Somewhere, too, you will find one or more fuses and these are rated at certain current values (in amps) and, at these values, they 'fuse' or open the circuit and stop the flow of electric current. Anti-surge fuses are more expensive than the normal ones but a great help if you are plagued by fuses blowing the moment you switch on.

DON'T FORGET : electricity can be lethal!

USEFUL ADDRESSES

Rick Wakeman Limited 3 Hill Street London W1

Halo Electrosound Limited Estuary House Exmouth Devon

British Society for Electronic Music 49 Deodar Road London SW15

Audio Engineering Society Inc 60 East 42nd Street New York NY 10017

Catgut Acoustical Society Inc 112 Essex Avenue Montclair NJ 07042

Industrial Tape Applications 5 Pratt Street London NW1

Watkins Electric Music Limited 66 Offley Road London SW9

Rupert Neve and Co Limited Cambridge House Melbourne Royston Herts

INDEX

Page references in italic indicate illustrations

167

ML
1092
J45
1976

Jenkins, John, 1936-

Electric music

58282